Other Books by Captain Rami Geffner, MD

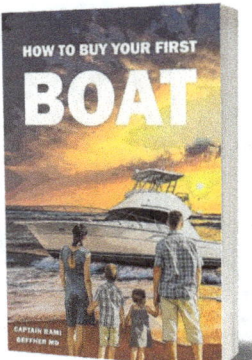

How to Buy Your First Boat is your essential guide to boat ownership. Discover how to assess your needs, set a budget, and explore different boat types. Learn about ownership costs, inspections, sea trials, and price negotiations. This book also provides valuable insights into the post-purchase process, ensuring you know what to do with your new or used boat. With practical advice and step-by-step instructions, *How to Buy Your First Boat* ensures you make informed decisions and enjoy smooth sailing.

Embark on an unforgettable voyage with Captain Rami Geffner aboard the Sea Scape, a Horizon PC60 power catamaran. This travelogue blends adventure, history, and personal anecdotes as it navigates from New Jersey's serene backwaters to Fort Lauderdale's vibrant shores. Discover America's coastline, maritime navigation challenges, and the joy of life at sea. Whether you're a seasoned sailor or an armchair traveler, *Intracoastal Voyage of the Sea Scape* promises to inspire and entertain with its vivid storytelling and practical insights.

Alaska Revealed

ALASKA
REVEALED

A GUIDE TO HOMER AND
THE ALAGNAK RIVER

CAPTAIN RAMI GEFFNER, MD

Imar Publishing

Copyright © 2025 by Captain Rami Geffner, MD

ISBN (Paperback): 979-8-9991712-0-7
ISBN (eBook): 979-8-9991712-1-4
ISBN (Audiobook): 979-8-9991712-2-1

Cover design and interior formatting by the Aaxel Author Group

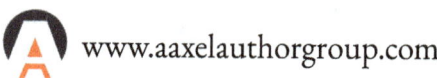 www.aaxelauthorgroup.com

To my parents and children
Sara and Herb
Jennifer, David, Victoria, Jonathan and Julianne

"Experience is what you get when you don't get what you want!"

Thank you for your love,
support, strength and confidence

CONTENTS

PREFACE

I returned to Alaska because I missed the entire experience, having visited twice before. Each time, the experience was entirely unique as I explored different places and engaged in new activities. I wish I had kept notes during those visits to better preserve the memories and reflect on them. I am certain that, because each trip was so distinct, I must have discovered things I've since forgotten, things I wish I could revisit and remember more clearly.

Determined not to let this current experience fade from memory, I decided to keep a journal of my daily adventures. In it, I not only captured the emotions and impressions each moment evoked but also documented questions that arose—things I wanted to learn more about and understand better. Beyond the physical and emotional aspects of my journey, I felt compelled to research and uncover the details behind everything I encountered.

I felt a deep desire and responsibility to give back, to ensure that my presence in Alaska was not just about taking but about honoring its unparalleled beauty, rich history, vibrant nature, incredible people, and the lush, thriving vegetation that breathes life into this land. Sharing the story of this extraordinary place is one of the most heartfelt ways I can express my gratitude for being welcomed into its embrace. This is not just a visit; it's a profound connection—a privilege I've cherished not only now but during the precious moments I've spent here before. To experience Alaska's majesty so intimately is a gift, and giving back in this way feels like the truest form of thanks.

Including the historical facts about Alaska, as I attempted to do, allowed me to better understand the environment I was in. As the trip progressed, I became increasingly aware that the people who conquered this land were only able to survive its harsh conditions by exploiting its resources, including birds, foxes, beavers, otters, and other wildlife. While this may have been necessary for survival at the time, things have changed. Today, our understanding and recognition of conservation have become far more important.

Human activity nearly led to the extinction of so many creatures in this region. Had we not come to our senses and implemented restrictions, we might have wiped out entire populations of these living beings. This realization became particularly evident during my visit to the visitor center in Homer, Alaska. The exhibits there explained these issues clearly and effectively. It's truly must-see.

CHAPTER 1

JULY 12

Before our trip to Alaska, we created a carefully thought-out plan. This plan made all the difference, transforming our adventure into an unforgettable experience. It proved so helpful that we'd like to share it with you.

THE FIRST LEG OF OUR JOURNEY

The first stop of our trip was a true off-the-grid gem: a fully self-sufficient lodge with its own electricity, clean water supply, and independent sanitation systems and even its own communication network. This beautiful lodge, nestled on the edge of the Alagnak River, combined rustic charm with remarkable ingenuity. It was surrounded by nothing but the river, dense vegetation, and abundant wildlife for miles. The closest city, King Salmon, was 40 miles away and could only be reached by seaplane—or bush plane—a journey that took about 30 to 45 minutes.

3

ALAGNAK LODGE
AND RIVER

FLIGHT ARRANGEMENTS

Reaching King Salmon was no straightforward task. There were no direct flights to our destination, so we started by taking Alaska Airlines from Newark, New Jersey (EWR) to Anchorage, Alaska, with a layover in Portland, Oregon. With six suitcases—packed with heavy winter clothing and fishing gear—our luggage was substantial, but Alaska Airlines handled everything seamlessly. All six pieces made it to King Salmon without a hitch.

We stayed overnight in Anchorage and continued to King Salmon the following morning on Ravn Alaska airline. When we arrived in King Salmon, our luggage, which had been checked in Newark, was waiting for us in perfect order—a testament to Alaska Airlines' efficiency.

4

As our journey progressed, the number of passengers on each flight dwindled. From Newark to Anchorage, about 150 passengers made the journey. From Anchorage to King Salmon, only 20 people were onboard. Finally, from King Salmon to the Alagnak Lodge, only four of us remained.

At King Salmon, we were met by a representative from Branch River Air, who drove us a short distance to the riverbank. Here, we boarded a small de Havilland Beaver plane, tightly packed with six pieces of luggage, four passengers, and the pilot.

Beaver plane to the Alagnak River

Alagnak River and Lodge (under plane).

Mount Hood Oregon, layover.

Anchorage Airport

The pilot instructed us to put on headphones to muffle the deafening roar of the engines. As the plane began gliding across the water, picking up speed, I couldn't help but worry about the extra weight. *Would we actually get airborne?* To my immense relief—and as if answering my prayers—we did. Hurray! We were flying!

The 30-minute flight took us over vast wilderness and winding rivers, with expansive tundras stretching far below. The time seemed to pass quickly, and soon we spotted the Alagnak Lodge nestled at the edge of the river.

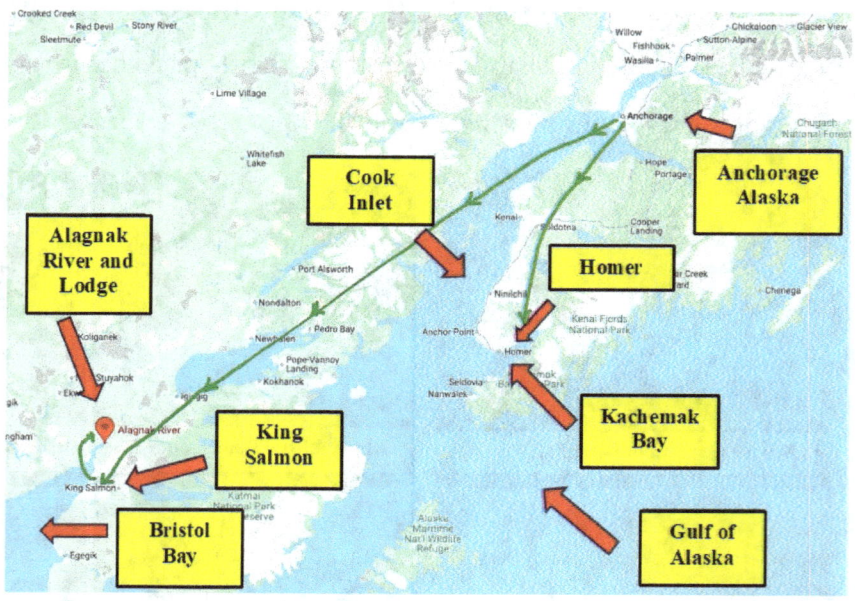

PACKING LIST

Here's what we packed to ensure we were prepared for our Alaskan adventure:

CLOTHING:

- Laundry is available on-site (washing machines and dryers)

- Waterproof hooded jacket suitable for cold and wet conditions
- Layered clothing for flexibility
- Thermal undergarments
- Appropriate footwear
- Gloves and a warm hat.

SUNDRIES:

- Prescription medicines
- Camera and chargers
- Insect repellent and sunscreen (or use the lodge's supplies)
- Polarized sunglasses
- Checks or cash for incidental expenses

FISHING GEAR AND EQUIPMENT (OR USE THE LODGE'S SUPPLIES):

- Waders and wading boots
- Rods and reels
- Terminal tackle and flies
- Fishing license

This plan ensured that we were ready for every aspect of the trip, allowing us to focus on enjoying the breathtaking beauty of Alaska and the Alagnak River.

CHAPTER 2

JULY 13

This was not our first time in Alaska. We had visited this magnificent land before, and its charm and grandeur had drawn us back once more. Every trip we've taken there has been unique, each one adding a new chapter to our ongoing saga of Alaskan adventures. This trip, too, promised to be distinct and unforgettable.

The history of Alaska has always fascinated me. The Alaska Purchase, finalized in 1867, transferred this vast territory from Russia to the United States for $7.2 million (equivalent to $129 million in 2023). The US Senate ratified the treaty on May 15, 1867, and American sovereignty became official on October 18 of that year.

Russia had established a colonial presence in parts of North America during the first half of the 18th century, but few Russians ever settled in Alaska. After suffering a devastating defeat in the Crimean War, Alexander II of Russia saw Alaska as indefensible in any future conflict and began exploring its sale. William H. Seward, then US secretary of state, negotiated with Russian diplomat Eduard de Stoeckl. Their agreement culminated in a treaty signed on March 30, 1867, which was after the American Civil War.

I once had the pleasure of treating William Seward's great-great-granddaughter as a patient. We had quite a conversation about her famous ancestor. It's incredible how connected we all are—proof of the saying "We are all linked by six degrees of separation." Or better yet, as I will explain later in the book, by a drop of water! What a small world!

Now, I'm excited all over again! In just a few days, I'll be back in Alaska. I can hardly contain my emotions. The last time I was there was just before the COVID-19 pandemic, and I've been yearning to return ever since. When I think of Alaska, I think of its pristine wilderness and peaceful stillness. I think of its soaring eagles, playful foxes, and majestic bears. There's nothing Alaska offers that I don't love.

Every time I've visited Alaska, I've left with a longing to stay longer and a burning desire to return. Whether exploring its mountains and glaciers, hiking its trails, watching bears feast on salmon, kayaking through its waters, or fishing in its rivers, Alaska never disappoints.

Spring and summer in Alaska are magical. The melting ice and snow awaken the plants, flowers, and wildlife. Birds and fish return to breed, while the stunning landscape seems to come alive. Alaska's seasons are distinct, and its daylight patterns are equally unique. Winters bring long, dark nights, especially in places like Utqiaġvik (formerly Barrow), where the sun doesn't rise for about 65 days. Conversely, summers offer the midnight sun, with 24 hours of daylight for roughly 82 days.

ON THE WAY TO ALASKA

As I sit on Alaska Airlines flight 283, which just departed Newark Liberty International Airport (EWR), I feel a mix of excitement and anticipation. The flight to Portland, Oregon (PDX) will take six hours and seven minutes, though we were delayed on the tarmac for 45 minutes. Perhaps the pilot can make up some time by speeding up the journey.

In my cushioned and comfortable seat, 34,000 feet above the ground, I have begun writing in my journal. It has been far too long since my last visit to Alaska. During the pandemic, travel restrictions kept me grounded, and I've been longing to reconnect with its wilderness, wildlife, and history ever since.

If all goes well, we'll spend the next nine days touring, exploring, and fishing along the Alagnak River. I hope to witness the sockeye salmon's second run before the chum salmon begin their migration upstream from Bristol Bay.

Packing for this trip felt like an endless task. Knowing we'd be in the wilderness, far from any commercial amenities or hospitals, I prepared for every possible situation. I packed a netted hat for mosquitoes, nontoxic repellents, and a full first-aid kit, including antibiotics, ointments, bandages, sutures, and even a battery-operated cautery. While I hoped these supplies would remain unused, I wanted to be ready for anything.

In addition to my medical supplies, I packed my MacBook Air, iPad, chargers, artificial fishing flies, and two eight-weight fly rods—perfect for the Alagnak River. I also brought lighter fishing gear and an assortment of warm, waterproof clothing for temperatures ranging from 50 to 60 degrees Fahrenheit. Four suitcases later, I was finally ready.

Mount Hood

As we flew toward Portland, the captain announced that Mount Hood would be visible on the left. What a thrill! Mount Hood, the highest point in Oregon at 11,245 feet, is a dormant volcano that last erupted in 1865. It's surrounded by Mount Hood National Forest, a haven for outdoor enthusiasts.

We landed in Portland without a hitch and spent a few hours there before boarding our next flight to Anchorage, Alaska.

Arrival in Anchorage

After touching down in Anchorage around 2 a.m., we navigated the quiet airport in search of a ride to the Ramada hotel downtown. The hotel shuttle was nowhere to be found, so we flagged a taxi. Exhausted, we checked into the hotel, only to find it less than ideal. After switching rooms twice due to a malfunctioning air conditioner, we finally settled in. Who would've thought we'd need air conditioning in Alaska?

Anchorage International Airport

Chapter 3

July 14

We caught a few hours of sleep and headed back to Anchorage International Airport in the early morning to catch another flight to King Salmon.

The airport in Anchorage is much smaller than Newark Liberty International Airport. Many of the jets there, besides those with Alaskan Air, were from Ravn Alaska. Ravn, pronounced like the bird raven, is an Alaskan airline specializing in serving small communities in Alaska. This airline is headquartered in that state.

The ride to King Salmon that day was uneventful. The weather was cold, in the 40s when we left, and it was raining. We landed in King Salmon in about 45 minutes, flying on a De Havilland Dash 8-300. It was not a Boeing or an Airbus by any stretch of the imagination but comfortable for a twin-turbo propeller plane.

We reached the tiny King Salmon Airport. The building consisted of one large room with an attached gift shop housed in a wooden structure. The building was packed with people, most of whom were looking for their next ride and scanning the crowd for drivers holding signs to identify their passengers. After a short while, we found our driver, who moved our luggage to his pickup truck and drove us about 10 minutes to a river.

Thereafter, battling down a long, steep ramp, we boarded an even smaller floatplane known as a De Havilland Beaver. No more twin-turbo propeller engines—now we were stepping into a single-propeller engine plane. It was tiny, holding at most the pilot, a passenger next to the pilot, and room for three average-sized people in the back row. Behind this row was the cramped space where all the luggage was squished in.

It was both exciting and a little scary. We were extremely cramped inside, with the luggage barely fitting behind us. We were given headsets to muffle the noise of the engine, but as we started to take off, I couldn't help but feel nervous. With all that weight on the plane, I worried we might never lift off. Deep inside, I was praying that we would make it out alive.

By now, late morning, the weather was cold, very windy, and still raining. As the engine roared and we wore our headsets, the plane began to gain speed on the river. Finally, the nose veered up, and we were a few hundred feet over the water.

Joining us in this very cramped plane were two other passengers from Switzerland, also heading to the Alagnak Lodge for the week.

I couldn't help but think, *Two more people and all this baggage in such a small plane—can we really make it?* We had a lot of blind faith that morning. The thought kept running through my mind: *What have I gotten us into?*

I sat in the left back seat of the plane, next to the window, counting down the next 30 minutes of flight and hoping we would land safely. As I stared out the window, all I could see below were undulating rivers, isolated little lakes, and endless stretches of fir and spruce trees. I kept thinking, *If this plane goes down and we survive, we'll surely be eaten by bears and wolves because there's nothing but water and wilderness for miles.*

But I tried to stay optimistic, whispering to myself that it wouldn't happen to us. To occupy my mind and calm my nerves, I continuously snapped pictures of the ground below. Even though I could barely turn my body in the cramped space, taking photos helped distract me and made the time pass a little faster.

After about 30 minutes, we began our descent toward the Alagnak River. I kept taking pictures and videos through the back window, even though I knew they would come out blurry and distorted. Most importantly, it gave me something to focus on besides my fear.

As the plane touched down on the river, the pontoons vibrated against the water's surface. Slowly, we made our way to a floating dock, where the plane was tied down. The dock was surrounded by flat-bottom johnboats with 40-horsepower Yamaha engines. Lodge employees were there to greet us and quickly began unloading our luggage from the plane.

Branch Air's beaver plane will be taking us to the Alagnak Lodge.

The Alagnak River and Lodge with its docks and Johnboats waiting for

Deplaning at the Alagnak Lodge dock.

Within a short time, they moved the luggage to the end of the dock, where they placed it on a makeshift stainless-steel elevator. The elevator, pulled by a stainless-steel cable, carried the luggage up the steep embankment. The embankment was so steep that a 48-step staircase was built next to the dumbwaiter for guests and employees to climb. Thankfully, none of us had to lug our bags up those steps—it would've been nearly impossible. I was so impressed with the elevator that I immediately began taking photos and videos as proof of its existence.

Climbing the 48 steps was quite a walk. I could feel the strain in my legs, my heavy breathing, and my racing heart. When I finally reached the top, there was a sign painted on a plaque that read "48 steps." To the right of the stairs, I noticed the gas-powered engine that drove the stainless-steel cable. I couldn't believe this small, lawnmower-like engine was powerful enough to pull such heavy loads up the embankment. It looked like an old dinosaur from prehistoric times, but it was a brilliant piece of simple engineering. Kudos to whoever came up with this idea—a clever invention that got the job done!

The makeshift elevator carrying luggage and other bulky, heavy materials was a unique structure. The 48 steps stood for the lower 48 states of the United States and were built alongside the elevator. The food was delicious.

At the top, the employees unloaded the luggage and carried it about 300 feet to the main lodge. After I marveled at the elevator, my attention shifted to the lodge itself. It was a white wooden building with a light-red metal seamless roof with a wooden walkway leading to a porch and then a few more steps to the entrance.

We climbed the steps and entered a vestibule—a mudroom where coats, hats, gloves, and boots could be left to dry. This room served as a buffer between the outdoors and the lodge's interior, keeping the main space clean and warm.

Once inside, we entered the great room, which immediately stood out as the heart of the lodge. This room served multiple purposes; it was the dining room, meeting area, and the main hub of communication. The kitchen was behind it, and a table against one wall held an assortment of condiments. Upstairs were the bedrooms, but this central room connected everyone.

This was where we would meet the staff, other guests, and our guides, discuss the lodge's itinerary and rules, and share stories between meals. Coffee and tea were always available, no matter the time of day or night. This was the start of what promised to be an unforgettable adventure.

Tony, the owner of the lodge, made this trip possible because of his tenacity, knowledge, dedication, and passion for Alaska. (upper left)

Matt on the right, and Peter his brother (down one to the left) were our guides and all-around great guys.

Other guests at the lodge from Switzerland on the bottom.

Dark Star their black Lab, gave the lodge a special homey feel. Bark Bark! Thank you.

ALAGNAK RIVER LODGE HISTORY

In July 1979, the four lodge founders camped 10 miles upriver on the Alagnak. They had fished at other lodges in Alaska, but the fishing on the Alagnak was the best they had ever experienced. To them, a tidal water location was ideal, so they arranged a lease on a 10-acre site just upriver from the present location. By this time, they had decided to build a lodge rather than continue camping.

A barge was loaded in Seattle, Washington, with building materials, boats, motors, and generators. With a crew of 14, construction began in May 1980 and was completed just in time for the first guests to arrive on July 4, 1980.

In 1992, a survey revealed that the lodge had been built in the wrong place, not quite on the land being leased. To resolve this, the lodge owners purchased 11 acres, and the lodge facility was moved to its current location, a short distance south of the original spot, closer to the mouth of the river. This monumental feat was accomplished over the fall and spring seasons and included bringing the lodge up to all current building codes.

In 1997, the current owner, Tony Behm, started the purchase process and assumed operations of the lodge. Since then, improvements and upgrades have been made periodically, including new staff quarters, infrastructure, boats, jet and prop motors, and a new dock. The lodge is now well-maintained and up to modern standards while remaining true to its roots as a fishing camp.

THE MISSION OF THE ALAGNAK LODGE

- To provide the Alaska wilderness lodge experience that their clients desire

- To respect the wilderness and minimize the environmental impact
- To act as caretakers of the land and coexist with the wildlife
- To ensure that the guests enjoyed their vacations and created memorable experiences tailored to their individual desires

The abundant wildlife, isolation, and tranquility of the river are what guests love most. Although at its core the lodge is a traditional fishing camp, it strives to meet the expectations of clients who desire a certain level of comfort and proficiency at the lodge and restaurant functions.

On the afternoon of July 14, we met Gavin Viohl, a young man from Charleston, South Carolina. This was Gavin's third season at the lodge. In his first two years, Gavin had been hired to help around the lodge with odd jobs, including assisting in the kitchen, washing dishes, cleaning, vacuum-packing fish, and acting as a general handyman. Over time, he gained the respect of the more tenured employees and eventually became a guide.

To qualify as a guide, Gavin had to earn his captain's six-pack license and complete additional paperwork required by the state of Alaska. At just 22 years old, Gavin was mature and confident. He would guide us twice daily on the river: a morning session from 7 a.m. to noon and an afternoon session from 1 p.m. to 6 p.m.

We noticed that Gavin preferred to return to the lodge for lunch, even if we didn't particularly care to leave the river. He enjoyed the camaraderie of the other guides, exchanging stories and observations from the morning's activities. We liked Gavin and wanted to ensure he was happy, so we accommodated this routine.

When we returned to the lodge, everyone—guests, guides, and even Tony—would eat together like one big family. It was a warm and welcoming experience.

OUR FIRST EXCURSION ON THE ALAGNAK RIVER

That afternoon, we climbed aboard a flat-bottomed johnboat powered by a 40-horsepower Yamaha outboard engine. The boat was completely open, leaving us fully exposed to the elements. This marked our introduction to the Alagnak River.

The weather was cold, rainy, and overcast. Not even a single fish jumped out of the water to make a splash, as they sometimes do. It was eerily quiet—you could hear a pin drop.

The surrounding vegetation was unfamiliar to us. As studiers of plants and trees, we would have loved to explore it more closely and identify what was growing around us, but today was not the day. The weather beat us down, and fatigue crept in, urging us not to linger. This was our first taste of the Alagnak River, a sobering introduction.

Despite our enthusiasm, the afternoon remained quiet. We

didn't catch any fish. The river was still, and the surrounding wilderness seemed dormant. After a couple of hours, we decided to head back to the lodge. There were no signs of birds, bears, or other wildlife.

When we returned, we ate a small dinner and went straight to our rooms. Exhausted from the day's long travel, the small beaver plane ride, and moving into the lodge, we fell into a deep sleep almost immediately.

The two other guests who had traveled with us from King Salmon were from Zurich, Switzerland. Both were very tall men. The father, Bruno, was a financier, and his son, John, was 16 years old. Bruno's mastery of the English language far surpassed John's, though both were able to communicate well enough.

In conversation, they explained that in Switzerland, their dialect differed slightly from old German. I was somewhat familiar with German, as my father was Austrian and often spoke it at home. I could tell that Bruno and John shared a close relationship.

Throughout the week, it was very nice to observe how well the two interacted. Their bond was strong and unwavering, a testament to their mutual respect and affection.

John and his father Bruno from Switzerland

For the most part, both Bruno and John kept to themselves and spent almost all their time together whenever they were seen. They would always sit next to each other during meals and occasionally find themselves directly across from us, giving us a chance to chat while eating. I would sometimes hear them laugh, especially John.

Bruno, on the other hand, appeared to be more serious than his son. He was always deeply focused on their conversations, giving the impression that they had little need for distraction from anyone else in the dining room. Frankly, I thought it was heartwarming to see their connection. Occasionally, Bruno would force a smile to appear cordial, but his presence was quite intimidating.

He was a big, tall, strapping man with a clean-shaven head, a well-built physique, and only a minimally protruding abdomen for his age. He appeared to be in his 50s, perhaps approaching 60. His commanding, deep, and naturally loud voice, paired with his expressive facial movements, made his demeanor unmistakable. One could easily read his mood just by watching his face.

I inferred that he was well off financially. During our stay, I learned that, in addition to having a career in banking, he also owned a large real estate management company. Our conversations were limited, as he seemed intent on keeping an eye on John and spending most of his time talking with him. If I had to guess, I'd say that perhaps they hadn't spent much time together in the past and that Bruno was trying to make up for lost moments.

That afternoon, we had the pleasant surprise of meeting Dark Star, a pedigreed black Labrador retriever, about 11 years old, who was adored by everyone at the lodge. Dark Star was the most well-behaved and entertaining dog we had ever met.

He had been trained as a diabetic detection dog, tasked with alerting his owner to dangerous levels of blood sugar. Mat and Peter are brothers both of whom worked as guides at the lodge. They lived in California in different regions. After Mat's father passed, Mat took ownership and responsibility for Dark Star. The two became inseparable and the best of friends. Dark Star had amazing skills, one of which was the ability to sense when a person's blood sugar became elevated and letting them know about this problem.

Mat has five brothers, one of whom is Peter. Peter was also staying at the lodge with us. Both Mat and Peter are phenomenally talented and hardworking with no lazy bones in their bodies. Peter was a natural problem solver, a seeker of knowledge who could fix or build just about anything mechanical he put his mind to.

Peter would challenge himself with new projects, even ones he'd never done before. He would master the task, finish it, and then move on to something new. He was a unique person, always ready to help anyone, whether it was someone at the lodge or a friend hundreds of miles away.

Mat, meanwhile, took care of Dark Star and lived off the grid. He and Peter were very close, often collaborating when Mat needed help with his stuff at the off-the-grid home. Using FaceTime, they worked through projects together, no matter the distance. Their friendship and brotherly bond were evident in everything they did.

By 8 p.m., we were all exhausted. It was our first day at the lodge, and we needed rest for whatever the next day would bring. We knew the next morning would start early, between 5 and 6 a.m. We hence wanted to be prepared for our first full day on the Alagnak River.

Dark Star was a very quiet dog. We never heard him bark during our entire stay at the lodge. Yet, his energy and grace were remarkable as he jumped into the Alagnak River to retrieve anything thrown for him. He swam like a duck, calm and smooth on the surface while paddling furiously underneath.

Watching him was mesmerizing. No branch was too big for him to chase and retrieve, even against the current. He did it effortlessly, clutching thick branches in his powerful jaws. Many times, I stopped in my tracks just to watch and admire him in his pursuit.

Even when the guides wrestled the chef to protect us all (a story I'll share later), Dark Star remained calm and silent. When I asked Mat if Dark Star ever barked, he chuckled and said, "You should hear him bark when he's chasing a bear up a tree."

Dark Star, Labrador retriever

CHAPTER 4

JULY 15

The Alagnak River begins in the Aleutian Range and, for the first six miles, winds through the tundra. A tundra is an area devoid of trees due to its frigid climate, but it is inhabited by various grasses. The river starts its outflow from Kukaklek Lake in Katmai National Park, in the northern part of the region, and flows south into Bristol Bay. Bristol Bay merges westwardly with the Bering Sea. The Alagnak Lodge is situated about five miles from the mouth of the river, where it opens into Bristol Bay and is located on the edge of the river.

The Alagnak River is a federally designated Wild and Scenic River that originates in Katmai National Park and Preserve. It's a fisherman's paradise and one of the most popular fishing float trips in the Bristol Bay region. From its headwaters at Kukaklek Lake or Nonvianuk Lake, the river stretches 75 miles and features a mix of Class I and II waters, with one Class III canyon a mile long that includes a short fall. It's a great destination for family and friends seeking a float trip centered around fishing. The upper river flows through the tundra, while the middle and lower reaches are lined with trees, creating varied and scenic landscapes.

This area is known for its mostly brown bears, which you are almost guaranteed to see while traveling the river. Due to its popularity, it's common to encounter many other travelers on the river. Many enjoy a wonderful six-day trip of moderate whitewater rapids, suitable for rafts and inflatable kayaks.

On this day we navigated the river in search of sockeye salmon, hoping to catch them during their second run. The first sockeye run occurred about three weeks before we arrived.

The Alagnak River, in Alaska's Bristol Bay area, is famous for its salmon runs, which attract both wildlife and fishing enthusiasts. Several species of salmon travel up this river during distinct periods, driven by their spawning cycles. Here's an overview of the salmon species and their typical timing:

KING SALMON (CHINOOK) (ALSO CALLED KINGS)

- **Timing:** Late June to early August
- **Details:** Chinook enters the river early in the summer. They are a prized catch for anglers due to their size and strength.

Chinook salmon possess many distinctive characteristics, including:

- **Size:** Chinook salmon are the largest Pacific salmon species, capable of growing over five feet long and weighing more than 100 pounds.
- **Color:** In the ocean, Chinook salmon are blue-green on their backs and silvery on their sides, with white bellies and black spots on their upper bodies and tailfins. As they prepare to spawn in freshwater, their coloration changes to shades of olive brown, red, or purple.
- **Features:** Chinook salmon have small eyes, black gum lines, and prominent teeth. Males develop hooked upper jaws and ridged backs, features that become most pronounced before spawning. Females have torpedo-shaped bodies, robust midsections, and blunt noses.
- **Migration:** Chinook salmon are anadromous, hatching in freshwater streams and rivers before migrating to the ocean to feed and grow. They can travel up to 3,000 miles (4,800 kilometers) to spawn, using the sun and their keen sense of smell to navigate back to their natal rivers.

- **Lifespan:** Chinook salmon can live up to eight years, giving them one of the longest lifespans among Pacific salmon species.

SOCKEYE SALMON (RED)

- **Timing:** Mid-June to mid-August
- **Details:** Sockeye runs are some of the most significant in the Alagnak, with large numbers of fish returning to spawn. This species is known for its vibrant red coloration during spawning.

SOCKEYE SALMON OVERVIEW

- **Appearance:** Sockeye salmon are a smaller species of Pacific salmon, typically measuring 1.5–2.5 feet in length and weighing 4–15 pounds. They have iridescent silver flanks, a white belly, and a metallic green-blue top, which is why they are also referred to as "blueback" salmon. However, when they return to their freshwater spawning grounds, their bodies transform into a bright red color with green heads, earning them the nickname "red" salmon.

- **Behavior:** Sockeye salmon are anadromous, meaning they hatch in freshwater before migrating to the ocean to feed and grow. They generally mature and return to freshwater after spending 2–3 years at sea, though some individuals may return earlier or remain in the ocean longer.

- **Spawning:** During spawning, male sockeye salmon develop a humped back and hooked jaws. Non-dominant males often act as satellites to mated pairs, positioning themselves nearby in hopes of spawning opportunities.

- **History:** Sockeye salmon were the first species of Pacific salmon to be harvested commercially and canned in large quantities, starting in the late 1870s. They played a foundational role in establishing the commercial salmon fishing industry.

- **Nutrition:** Sockeye salmon are highly nutritious, providing an excellent source of omega-3 fatty acids and astaxanthin, a powerful antioxidant that gives their flesh its vibrant pink color.

- **Commercial Importance:** Sockeye salmon are a cornerstone of North American commercial fisheries. Their concentrated run timing, firm flesh, and rich flavor made them a popular choice for canning and continue to make them a valuable species in commercial markets today.

Chum Salmon (Dog)

Chum Salmon Overview

- **Timing:** Chum salmon make two spawning runs each year—the first begins in mid-July and continues through August, while the second occurs from February to March.
- **Details:** Chum salmon are an important species for the ecosystem, contributing significantly to the food chain for both wildlife and humans.

The chum salmon is easily recognized by the wide striations on its body, is a unique species of Pacific salmon. It exhibits several distinctive characteristics:

- **Appearance:** In the ocean, chum salmon have a metallic greenish-blue coloration with black speckles. When they enter freshwater to spawn, their appearance undergoes a dramatic transformation:
    - *Males:* Develop a calico-like pattern, featuring a reddish line on the front two-thirds of their flank and a black line along the back third. They also grow large, canine-like teeth and a hooked snout.
    - *Females:* Turn brown to gray, with a broad, dark horizontal bar along their sides. They too develop canine-like teeth, but less prominently than the males.
- **Size:** Chum salmon can reach lengths of up to 3.6 feet and weigh as much as 45 pounds, though their average weight typically ranges from 8 to 15 pounds.
- **Tail:** A defining feature of chum salmon is its highly forked tail, which has silver streaks running along the fin rays.
- **Lifespan:** On average, chum salmon live three to five years, though some individuals may spend as long as seven years at sea before returning to spawn. Most chum

salmon, however, remain in the ocean for about four years.

- **Habitat:** Chum salmon are usually found in watersheds near the saltwater coast and are less likely to inhabit waterways far inland. They prefer small coastal streams and the lower reaches of larger rivers.

- **Spawning:** Chum salmon spawn from November through late December. During this time, they are capable of incredible feats of migration, swimming more than 3,200 kilometers (2,000 miles) up the Yukon River to reach their spawning grounds.

- **Nickname:** Chum salmon are often called "dog salmon," a reference to the large canine-like teeth that males develop during spawning.

PINK SALMON (HUMPY)

- **Timing:** There are two distinct , reproductively isolated populations of pink salmon that spawn in alternate years.

This is due to their strictly two-year life cycle. Odd-year and even-year populations do not interbreed, even when they spawn in the same rivers.

The pink salmon, often identified by its prominent humpback, spends only about 18 months at sea before returning to freshwater to spawn. Here are some characteristics of pink salmon:

Unlike coho, Chinook, or sockeye salmon, pink salmon do not reside in freshwater for extended periods. Once they reach the ocean, they feed voraciously and grow rapidly, making them one of the fastest-growing Pacific salmon species.

- **Size:** Pink salmon are the smallest Pacific salmon in North America, typically weighing 3.5–5 pounds and measuring 20–25 inches in length.
- **Color:** In the ocean, pink salmon are steel blue to blue-green on their backs, silver on their sides, and white on their bellies. As they approach spawning streams, males turn dark on their backs and develop red sides with brownish-green blotches. Females, by contrast, turn olive green with dusky bars or patches that may appear lavender or dark gold.
- **Spots:** Large, oval-shaped black spots are visible on their backs and on both lobes of their tails.
- **Hump:** Breeding males develop a pronounced hump on their backs, which gives pink salmon their nickname:

"humpback" salmon.

- **Jaws:** Males develop a hooked jaw, known as a kype.
- **Mouth:** Pink salmon have a white mouth with a black gumline and tongue.
- **Scales:** Pink salmon are characterized by their very small scales.
- **Lifespan:** Pink salmon have the shortest lifespan of all Pacific salmon in North America, completing their entire life cycle—from hatching to spawning—within two years.
- **Spawning:** Females create nests, called redds, in the riverbed, where they lay between 1,200 and 1,900 eggs. Like all Pacific salmon, pink salmon die after spawning.
- **Range:** Pink salmon are native to the Pacific and Arctic coastal waters and rivers, ranging from the Sacramento River in California to the Mackenzie River in Canada.

COHO SALMON (SILVER)

- **Timing:** August to late October

- **Details:** Coho salmon runs extend later into the season. Known for their aggressive nature, these salmon are popular among anglers.

Coho salmon, also known as silver salmon, have several notable characteristics, including:

- **Appearance:** Coho salmon have dark blue or green backs, silver sides, and light-colored bellies. In the ocean, they display small black spots on their backs and the upper lobes of their tails. When they return to freshwater to spawn, their appearance changes to dark backs and reddish-maroon sides. Spawning males develop hooked snouts and large teeth.

- **Size:** Coho salmon are typically 24–30 inches long and weigh 8–12 pounds. However, they can grow up to 42 inches in length and weigh as much as 36 pounds.

- **Habitat:** Coho salmon inhabit the Pacific coasts of California, Oregon, Washington, British Columbia, and Alaska. They can migrate hundreds of miles inland to spawn in tributaries of the Columbia and Snake rivers. Some populations, known as landlocked, spend their entire lives in freshwater.

- **Lifecycle:** Coho salmon spend 1–3 years in saltwater before returning to freshwater to spawn. Their eggs hatch in late winter or early spring and remain in the redd for six to seven weeks. Once the yolk sac is absorbed, the alevin leaves the redd and spends 1–2 years in freshwater. Smolts migrate to the ocean between late March and July.

- **Spawning:** Female coho salmon can lay between 2,400 and 4,500 eggs. The spawning season runs from mid-October through early January.

PEAK SALMON RUNS BY MONTH

- **June:** Start of king and sockeye runs
- **July:** Peak for sockeye, chum, and pink salmon (in odd years)
- **August:** Strong runs for coho, with lingering sockeye, chum, and king
- **September/October:** Coho dominates as other species taper off

The exact timing of runs can vary yearly due to environmental factors such as water temperature and flow. Planning a visit for fishing or sightseeing, local resources or guides can provide up-to-date information for the season.

Differences between Atlantic and Pacific salmon lie mostly in their spawning behavior. Unlike Pacific salmon, which die after spawning, Atlantic salmon survive and can return to the ocean, allowing them to respawn in subsequent years repeatedly.

The difference in their ability to survive is a fascinating phenomenon and highlights the unique strategies of these two species.

1. Life Cycle and Spawning Behavior

- *Atlantic Salmon:* Atlantic salmon are *iteroparous*, meaning they can spawn multiple times throughout their lives. After spawning, they return to the ocean to recover and may spawn again in future years.

- *Pacific Salmon:* Pacific salmon are *semelparous*, meaning they spawn only once and die shortly afterward. Their reproductive strategy focuses on a single, massive spawning effort.

2. Physiological Changes

- *Energy Investment:* Pacific salmon undergo dramatic physiological changes during spawning, expending nearly all their energy reserves, leading to rapid deterioration.

- *Post-Spawning Decline:* After spawning, Pacific salmon experience muscle breakdown, fat depletion, and heightened vulnerability to disease, ultimately causing their death.

3. **Evolutionary Strategies**

- *Atlantic Salmon:* By spawning multiple times, Atlantic salmon spread their reproductive success across several seasons, adapting to favorable conditions.

- *Pacific Salmon:* Pacific salmon invest all their reproductive energy into one event, producing a large number of eggs to ensure survival in unpredictable environments.

4. **Habitat and Migration Patterns**

- *Atlantic Salmon:* They migrate back to the ocean after spawning, where abundant food resources help them regain their strength.

- *Pacific Salmon:* After their single spawning event, Pacific salmon do not return to the ocean, as their life cycle ends.

SALMON LIFE CYCLE STAGES

Salmon undergoes a series of distinct stages in their life cycle, transitioning from freshwater to saltwater and back. This process can take 2–3 years after hatching.

1. **Egg Stage**

- Salmon eggs are laid in gravel nests called *redds* in

freshwater streams or rivers. These small, translucent to orange or pink eggs incubate for 60–100 days, depending on water temperature.

2. Alevin Stage

- Upon hatching, alevins remain in the gravel, feeding on nutrients stored in their yolk sacs for several weeks.

3. Fry Stage

- Once the yolk sac is absorbed, fry begin swimming freely and feed on small aquatic insects and zooplankton.

4. Parr Stage

- Fry develop into parr, characterized by distinctive dark vertical markings that provide camouflage. They stay in freshwater for 1–3 years, depending on species and

5. Smolt Stage

- Smolts undergo a process called smoltification, adapting to life in saltwater. They lose their parr markings and develop a silvery coloration, preparing for migration to the ocean.

6. Adult Stage

- In the ocean, adult salmon grow significantly, feeding on marine organisms. After maturing, they return to their natal rivers to spawn.

7. Kelt Stage (Atlantic Salmon only)

- Post-spawning Atlantic salmon, or kelts, return to the ocean to recover and may spawn again in future years. This stage is absent in Pacific salmon, whose life cycle ends after spawning.

Today, as we explore the Alagnak River, these life cycle stages and behaviors remind us of the delicate balance of nature and the resilience of salmon. We hope to witness the sockeye salmon's journey firsthand, adding another layer of appreciation to our Alaskan adventure.

Because each of these stages is critical to the life cycle of salmon, it is important to understand it.

Salmon Life Cycle

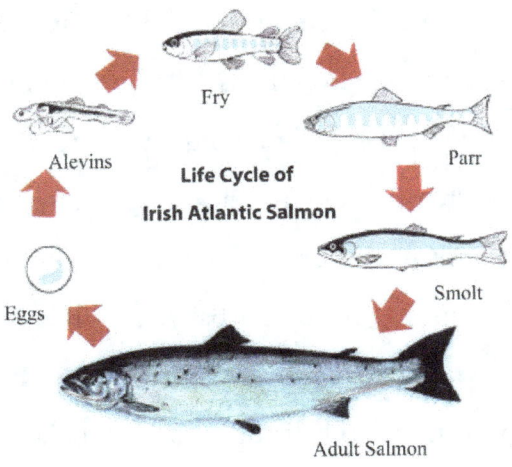

Are there enough reasons to justify sacrificing the Atlantic salmon population for the advantage of the Pacific salmon, given their reproductive differences?

The answer is no, and the following are the reasons:

1. **Population Vulnerability and Recovery**

   Atlantic salmon populations are significantly lower and more vulnerable compared to many Pacific salmon stocks. While Atlantic salmon can spawn multiple times (*iteroparous*), overfishing them places additional stress on already declining populations, severely limiting their ability to recover. Many Atlantic salmon populations are endangered or have faced sharp declines due to factors such as habitat loss, climate change, and pollution.

2. **Ecological Roles and Habitat Differences**

   Atlantic and Pacific salmon fulfill different ecological roles in their respective environments. Pacific salmon, which spawn once and then die (*semelparous*), provide vital nutrients to their ecosystems through their carcasses after spawning. This nutrient influx supports freshwater and terrestrial species, creating a unique ecological balance. While Atlantic salmon ecosystems do not depend on this same nutrient cycle, reducing their populations still disrupts food webs and local ecology, leading to far-reaching consequences.

3. Life Cycle Pressures and Overfishing Risks

Atlantic salmon already face intense pressures throughout their life cycle, including commercial fishing, habitat degradation, and competition with invasive species. Adding further fishing pressure could push these populations to critically low levels, threatening their long-term sustainability. Despite their ability to spawn multiple times, the stress of repeated captures, along with other environmental challenges, makes each spawning event increasingly precarious for their survival.

4. Genetic and Biodiversity Concerns

Atlantic salmon stocks have become genetically fragmented and isolated, leading to reduced genetic diversity and resilience. Overfishing exacerbates this problem, further diminishing their genetic pool. This limits their ability to adapt to changing environmental conditions and increases the risk of population collapse, posing a threat to the overall biodiversity of the species.

The sockeye salmon were the fish we had been waiting for to swim up the river from Bristol Bay. This would be their second run, returning from the ocean to hatch or fertilize their offspring and then die. It is said that only up to 10 percent of their offspring survive, eventually maturing in the river over three years before returning to the ocean. It is quite a process.

During this time in the river, their color changes dramatically.

Their bodies turn red and their heads become green, which is why they are also known as red salmon. When returning to spawn, they are no longer interested in eating. Instead, they rely on stored nutrients they consumed before making their long journey to the spawning grounds.

By the time they reach the river, after traveling hundreds of miles, avoiding predators, and not eating when they enter the river, their energy is nearly depleted while swimming up the river. Their bodies begin to deteriorate as a result. The closer they get to their spawning grounds, the more their color changes, and signs of their deterioration become evident.

This decline is visible throughout their bodies. Their skin starts to peel and rot and ulcerates, forming small shallow depressions where skin is missing. Their color fades, and their snouts become thin, bent, and arched like a proboscis. They become pointy rather than stay round as they once were. The roofs of their mouths and tongues take on a metallic appearance.

By this stage, they look very different from their original appearance—ugly and disfigured, with red bodies and green heads. Both males and females experience these changes because they put so much energy into the spawning process, sacrificing their own lives in the process.

We have observed these transformations while fishing on the Alagnak River. It is amazing to see the difference between what they looked like before and what some of them look like now. It is a major transformation that ultimately leads to their death.

BREAKFAST AND THE MORNING FISHING TRIP

This morning, we ate breakfast at 6:30 a.m., prepared by Chef Robert. Robert is a very outgoing, talented, and imaginative individual. He approaches life and cooking with enthusiasm. Completely unabashed and uninhibited. Just about everything that comes to his mind seems to find its way out of his lips.

He speaks from the heart, often without filters between his thoughts and words. While this can sometimes be a double-edged sword, neither Lauri nor I were ever offended by anything he said or did. We were both very fond of Chef Robert. He was extremely entertaining and entirely unpretentious.

This morning, Robert made one of my favorite breakfasts—biscuits and gravy—and I was very pleased. After finishing breakfast, we gathered our gear and followed our guide Gavin to the dock. I was dressed in a few layers of clothes for the day, due to my insecurity of becoming too cold. The temperature was in the mid-40s, expected to rise into the low 50 later in the day.

The dock at the Alagnak Lodge

We walked down the 48 steps to the floating dock, where our boat awaited us. There she was, an 18-foot flat aluminum johnboat powered by a 40-horsepower Yamaha engine.

After stepping aboard, Lauri and I took our seats in the two swivel chairs bolted to the floor. Gavin started the engine without a hitch, and we began our journey upriver, heading north—away from the mouth of the river.

We had been told at the lodge that the southern portion of the river, closer to the mouth, could be tricky to navigate due to shoaling and shallowness. As a safety precaution, guides were not permitted to travel more than a mile south of the lodge, toward the mouth. The lodge itself is situated approximately five miles from the river's mouth.

As we traveled, we passed a few other boats fishing slightly south of us, but the majority of the activity was to the north. Most of the boats spotted had traveled a good distance to fish closer to our lodge than theirs. Many of them came from the Katmai Lodge.

THE KATMAI LODGE

The Katmai Lodge was founded around 1979. It began as a small camp with just a few guides, but the area's excellent fishing conditions allowed it to grow steadily over the years. Eventually, it became larger and more of a permanent lodge.

Given how remote the locations of both the Alagnak and Katmai lodges are, receiving basic materials was a significant challenge. All building supplies, equipment, and food had to be shipped in a container by barge from Seattle to Naknek, Alaska. Once the materials arrived in Naknek, another barge was used to drop the container at the Alagnak River.

These trips were monumental tasks, often requiring around-the-clock effort from all staff members. The teamwork and coordination it took to transport these materials was impressive.

Our johnboat, by contrast, was incredibly faster and more efficient because we could travel at 35 mph in a fairly comfortable and safe manner. Unlike fishing in the ocean, there were no waves to contend with on the river. However, the tide changes were dramatic—up to 18 feet daily, with the potential of reaching as much as 25 feet.

Especially during high tides, as long as we could avoid drifting branches in the water, we could travel as fast as we liked. The smoothness of the ride and the power of the boat made navigating the river an exhilarating experience.

As we traveled north, a bold eagle with its partner came into view on a branch atop a towering spruce tree. Not far away we could see its nest with a peeping baby eagle inside. The sight was stunning: regal birds, sitting proudly, scanning the river for prey. Their strength and confidence were palpable, a sight both inspiring and humbling.

Beyond the river's edge we were surrounded by mostly evergreens. Nearly no deciduous trees were in sight, which caused me to turn my attention to the towering spruces. I was curious about the differences between the two species because I was unsure as to whether I was looking at a spruce tree or a fir, which dominated the landscape. My curiosity led me to try to ascertain their differences.

DIFFERENCES BETWEEN FIR AND SPRUCE TREES IN ALASKA

Fir and spruce trees share the Alaskan landscape but are distinguishable by several unique characteristics:

1. **Needle Shape and Texture**
   - Fir Trees: Flat, soft needles that do not roll between fingers. Needles are arranged like little combs on branches.
   - Spruce Trees: Sharp, stiff, four-sided needles that roll easily between fingers.

2. **Needle Attachment**
   - Fir Trees: Needles attach to branches with suction cup-like bases, creating a flat arrangement.
   - Spruce Trees: Needles attach with woody pegs, leaving rough branch textures after needles fall.

3. **Cone Characteristics**

- Fir Trees: Upright cones that disintegrate on the tree, leaving stems behind.

- Spruce Trees: Hanging cones that fall to the ground intact, making them easy to spot.

4. **Bark Texture**

- Fir Trees: Smooth bark with resin-filled blisters on young trees.

- Spruce Trees: Rough, flaky bark that becomes more pronounced with age.

5. **Growth Habitat and Size**

- Fir Trees: Commonly found in mountainous regions, generally smaller in stature.

- Spruce Trees: Thrive in boreal forests and coastal areas. Sitka spruce, in particular, can grow to massive sizes.

SPRUCE DOMINANCE ALONG THE ALAGNAK RIVER

Research revealed that spruce trees are more abundant along the Alagnak River than firs. The river flows through diverse landscapes—tundra, boreal forest, and wetlands—where white and black spruce dominate. These trees thrive in boreal and riparian zones, tolerating wet, waterlogged soils, particularly black spruce.

BOREAL FORESTS: THE TAIGA BIOME

The boreal forest, or taiga, is Earth's largest terrestrial biome, covering vast areas of Canada, Alaska, Russia, and Scandinavia. It plays a crucial role in global climate regulation and carbon storage.

1. **Climate**
   - Long, cold winters; short, mild summers.
   - Trees and plants adapt to extreme light variations and a short growing season.

2. **Tree Species**
   - Predominantly conifers like spruce, pine, and fir, which conserve water with frost-resistant needles.
   - Deciduous species like birch and aspen appear in less harsh areas.

3. **Soil and Vegetation**
   - Nutrient-poor, acidic soils due to slow decomposition.
   - Understory includes mosses, lichens, and shrubs like blueberries and cranberries.

4. **Wildlife**
   - Home to moose, wolves, lynx, bears, foxes, and numerous migratory bird species.

5. **Ecological Role**
   - Major carbon sink, absorbing more carbon than it releases.

- Supports biodiversity and regulates climate by affecting temperature and precipitation.

WHAT IS A BIOME?

A biome is a large geographic area defined by specific climate conditions, plant life, and wildlife. It functions as a distinct ecosystem shaped by temperature, precipitation, and geography.

- **Terrestrial Biomes:** Include tundras, deserts, grasslands, temperate forests, tropical rainforests, and boreal forests.
- **Aquatic Biomes:** Include freshwater ecosystems like lakes and rivers as well as marine ecosystems like oceans and reefs.

CARBON SEQUESTRATION IN BOREAL FORESTS

Boreal forests are critical for storing carbon and mitigating climate change.

1. **Tree Carbon Storage**
   - Trees absorb CO_2 through photosynthesis, storing it in wood and roots, reducing atmospheric CO_2.

2. **Soil Carbon Storage**
   - Organic material decomposes slowly in cold conditions, trapping carbon in the soil.

3. **Climate Regulation**

   • Dense canopies reduce surface temperatures and regulate Earth's albedo (sunlight reflection).

4. **Risks**

   • Wildfires, deforestation, and permafrost thaw release stored carbon, exacerbating climate change.

Exploring the Alagnak River and its surrounding boreal biome was a profound experience. Witnessing the interplay of life—from towering spruce trees to the transformation of sockeye salmon—offered a deeper appreciation for Alaska's ecological significance. These interconnected systems remind us of the delicate balance necessary to sustain life on Earth.

FISHING SUCCESS: FLOSSING SOCKEYE SALMON

As we continued upriver, Lauri broke the ice by flossing the first sockeye salmon of the day. Flossing is a fishing technique used to catch salmon swimming upstream to spawn. It involves using a long leader line to drift the hook naturally through the water, snagging the fish in the mouth. We had to study this technique as quickly as we could to catch some salmon swimming upstream on their run to or from the spawning grounds where their intent was to dig a nest in the river's gravel to form what we call a redd where the eggs would be spawned and fertilized.

Flossing Is an Artful Technique

It's a common method for catching salmon, leveraging their swimming behavior:

1. **Technique**

   - We used a long leader line about six feet with a sinker to guide a bare hook or feathered lure through the fish's open mouth.

   - We would cast upstream and allow the current to carry the line, ensuring it passed naturally through the water.

2. **Legal Hooking**

   - The fish must be hooked in the mouth to be legally caught. But let's be real: That does not occur 100 percent of the time, and the fish ends up getting hooked sometimes wherever on the body. When hooked in the mouth, where it is supposed to be, reeling the fish in is a lot easier on both the fish and the fisherman.

Lauri quickly perfected the technique, catching most of our haul that day. By the end of our outing, we had caught our limit of sockeye salmon. Gavin filleted the fish back at the lodge, revealing their vibrant orange meat—a color so bright it was almost unreal.

As Gavin was filleting the fish, Lauri and I walked up the 48 steps to the main lodge and joined the other guests and guides for dinner. Chef Robert prepared an incredible meal, baking some sockeye salmon with a mayonnaise-based sauce that was absolutely delicious. For dessert, he served a very tasty banana pie, unlike any I'd ever had before.

Robert had a cheerful demeanor, letting his emotions hang freely. It was easy to tell if he was happy, sad, or just plain pissed off—he didn't hide his feelings from anyone. His openness made him all the more entertaining, and Lauri and I thoroughly enjoyed his personality.

During dinner, I struck up a conversation with Peter Van Ginkle, a smart and strong Irishman in his 40s who worked as an electrician by trade. We bonded over a discussion about my boat, the *Sea Scape*, which had been giving me trouble with electrical issues, which I still hadn't figured out. Peter, the go-to person at the lodge for solving problems, seemed like the perfect person to offer helpful advice.

Peter had an impressive sense of responsibility, ensuring that everything at the lodge was in good operational condition. Since the lodge was off the grid, it had to be entirely self-sufficient, relying on two diesel generators to supply electricity. Peter explained that these generators provided 120 volts, with alternating wires set up to create an alternating current. One generator served as a backup in case the other failed.

He showed me pictures of a previous incident where burned wires had shut down one of the generators. Peter took on the task of replacing the wires himself and explained how he'd repaired the damage to restore power.

Peter was clearly proud of his work, and rightfully so. He shared pictures of a gas fireplace he had built for a friend, describing how he had run pipes underground to complete the system. His drive for knowledge and ability to repair nearly anything made him an indispensable member of the lodge's team. From maintaining outboard engines to fixing equipment, Peter embraced challenges with an open mind and sought out the knowledge required to succeed.

The lodge had six operable boats, and Peter ensured they ran like well-oiled machines. His confidence and expertise extended to repairing engines for friends back home in San Diego as well. When he wasn't guiding guests, he was the head maintenance man, tackling repairs and upkeep with the respect and admiration of the entire staff.

The Lodge's Operations and Challenges

The lodge opened in June and closed before the end of September each year, which brought its own set of challenges. Boats had to be pulled out of the river and onto the banks to prevent them from floating away during winter's high tides. Engines had to be winterized, a monumental task given the weight of the boats and engines.

Tony and his crew designed a makeshift crane bolted to the dock, along with a metal container, to help with the process. The crane lifted the boats and engines out of the water, placing the engines upright on stands for storage. The container, which functioned as a secure warehouse, was locked until spring.

Winterizing the lodge involved draining hoses, preparing the pumps that brought water from the river, and securing all equipment. In May or June, depending on the weather, the staff returned to reverse the process, setting up boats, engines, and utilities for the season.

Unfortunately, they often found evidence of break-ins upon returning. Vandals would steal everything from cutlery to electrical appliances, leaving a mess behind that required cleaning, repairs, and reordering supplies. Since the area was so remote, replacing stolen items was a time-consuming and expensive ordeal. Supplies had to be shipped to King Salmon and flown to the lodge, adding to the complexity. It is painstaking to get the entire lodge ready for the arrival of the first guests. Besides the difficulty of replacing stolen or missing items, the process of reordering is complicated and time-consuming. Unlike simply loading items into a car and driving them to the lodge, everything must be flown in by small planes, which is both costly and logistically challenging. Many necessities have to be shipped to King Salmon first, then flown to the lodge, adding to the expense and delays.

I cannot imagine the amount of effort, time, frustration, and money it takes to prepare this place. This is why I thanked Tony Behm, the owner of the lodge, and his staff repeatedly. Without his efforts and theirs, none of us would have been able to enjoy this unique place. I understand the immense effort required to keep everything running smoothly.

During this time, the lodge had only four guests, including us, although it would usually host 12 guests. This lightened the workload for the crew, as no new guests were scheduled to arrive until the end of July, long after we would be gone. We were set to leave on July 23.

Tony made plans to keep the employees busy during this lull. He tasked them with rebuilding the deck on the main house. Tony was meticulous, hardworking, and honest, traits that had kept the lodge running for so many years.

Tony also wanted the main lodge repainted. Previously, the lodge had been white with a red metal roof, giving it a charming, gingerbread-house appearance. However, the staff told me, Tony decided to change the color to a bright, deep green, a choice of color they did not prefer. Despite their reluctance, they respected Tony enough to carry out his vision.

The crew admitted they were cringing at the idea of painting the lodge green, but their respect for Tony and the tradition of the lodge meant they couldn't refuse. On top of that, none of them liked painting or setting up scaffolds. Enthusiasm for this particular job was low. Gavin and Glenn, the other guides at the lodge, who cared for the German guests, were exempt from the task due to their guiding duties, which made them happy.

ADJUSTING TO ALASKAN DAYS

The sun didn't set at the Alagnak until midnight, which was 4 a.m. back in New Jersey. This threw off my sleep schedule completely. I struggled to stay awake and knew it would take weeks to fully acclimate. Exhausted, I finally gave in and went to bed, hoping I'd adjust quickly to the long Alaskan days ahead.

Lauri with a sockeye salmon.

Gavin our guide cleaning the salmon.

CHAPTER 5

JULY 16

We woke up early and made our way from the second floor, where all the guest rooms were located, down to the first. The first floor housed the mess hall and all the facilities, including the restrooms. It was a bit inconvenient having to go downstairs to use the bathroom, but considering that we were essentially in the middle of nowhere, it was understandable. The irony of walking downstairs half-asleep just to find a restroom was not lost on us.

At the bottom of the stairs was the mess hall, a large and unpretentious room. At first glance, it was obvious this was where food was served. Pots and pans hung on the wall in the kitchen, visible through a doorway that separated it from the dining area. The dining room itself was filled with simple tables surrounded by padded chairs. One table was set aside with snacks for anyone to grab throughout the day.

The room served multiple purposes, doubling as a space for crew meetings, gatherings of guests, or discussions with the owner. It was a communal area where people came together to share meals, conversations, and plans for the day ahead.

BREAKFAST AT THE LODGE

Breakfast began at 6:30 a.m. and was always delicious. The spread included sausages, home fries, pancakes, and a variety of baked desserts, along with water, orange juice, and cranberry juice. Notably absent, however, was fresh fruit, which was understandable given the challenge of transporting perishable items to such a remote location.

The one disappointment for me was the lack of Sweet'N Low. As someone who relies on it to sweeten my coffee, I found its absence significant. I wish I could give it up because I know the consequence of its unhealthy nature, but then that would make me almost perfect, which is not what I am looking for. The lodge staff assured me they'd ordered it for me, but it never arrived because the grocery store in King Salmon didn't have it in stock. I found it hard to believe that an entire town, no matter how small or remote, would not carry such a precious item, but then it is what it is! For the next 11 days, I unfortunately drank my coffee with its bitter edge, longing for the familiar comfort of my two daily cups sweetened just right.

THE MORNING WALK TO THE DOCK

After breakfast, we headed down the 48 steps to the dock. As I descended, I noticed the steep incline of the ramp leading from the embankment to the floating dock. The drastic change in water level between high and low tide was remarkable.

Here, the tides could vary by as much as 18 feet or more. When the tide was high, much of the riverbank was hidden, but at low tide, the exposed landscape revealed a completely different scene. It was an incredible transformation, one that highlighted the power and beauty of this unique environment. Below is some of the more common representative vegetation along the banks.

Bluejoint Reed Grass

Fowl Blue Grass

Tufted Hair Grass

Bluejoint Reed Grass

Beaked Sedge Grass

Beaked Sedge Grass Enlarged

Slough Sedge Grass

Lyngbye's Sedge Grass

By the time we stepped into the johnboat, it was close to 7:30 a.m. Gavin started the engine, and we raced upriver while sitting comfortably in our small swivel chairs. Today, we were waiting for the sockeye salmon run, and luck was on our side—the salmon were just beginning their journey upriver.

The run had started because the Alaskan government had ordered the commercial fishing boats at the mouth of the Alagnak River to raise their nets for the next two days, allowing the salmon to enter the river. Using various techniques to measure the number of salmon entering the river, the government dictates the fishing activities at the river's mouth, deciding when nets can be lowered or raised. This control ensures enough salmon swim upstream to spawn and sustain future generations.

If the salmon counts fall below the expected average, the commercial boats are required to pull their nets until the numbers recover. Once the count improves, the boats are allowed to resume fishing. This tight regulation is critical; a significant decrease in salmon numbers could threaten future populations.

Even with the nets raised, the salmon face other dangers as they swim upriver. They must navigate shallow waters, shoals, and the river's strong currents. High tide offers their best chance for success, as the rising water helps them overcome obstacles like mud, gravel, stones, and shoals.

Swimming upriver is no easy feat for salmon, who embark on this grueling journey just to reproduce and die. The lower part of the river is especially treacherous, with stronger currents that can sweep eggs into the bay, where they become easy prey. To maximize survival, salmon aim to lay their eggs as far upriver as possible, where the calmer waters offer their offspring a better chance. Even so, out of the 1,500 to 10,000 eggs laid, only about 10 will survive to maturity. These odds are sobering, making every effort by the salmon a testament to their survival instincts.

A CLOSE ENCOUNTER WITH A BROWN BEAR

As we turned north, we spotted our first brown bear swimming across the Alagnak River. Hearing the roar of our engine—amplified in the otherwise silent environment—the bear hastened to reach the riverbank. Scrambling up the shore, he disappeared into the sagebrush as we passed his crossing point. I needed to know more about the nature and characteristics of both brown and black bears because even though we were in mostly a brown bear territory, I knew it was possible that we would come across a black bear too.

BROWN BEARS

Brown bears are one of the largest and most widely distributed bear species in the world, known for their strength, adaptability, and iconic status. Below is a detailed breakdown of their characteristics:

PHYSICAL CHARACTERISTICS

1. **Size**

   - **Length:** 5–9 feet (1.5–2.8 meters) from nose to tail
   - **Height at shoulders:** 3.5–4 feet (1–1.2 meters) when on all fours; up to 8 feet (2.4 meters) while standing upright
   - **Weight:**
     - Males (boars): 300–1,500 pounds (136–680 kg), depending on region and season
     - Females (sows): 200–800 pounds (91–363 kg)
     - Coastal brown bears (e.g., Kodiak bears) are significantly larger than inland bears due to abundant food sources like salmon.

2. **Coloration**

   - Fur ranges from light blond to dark brown or almost black
   - Often have a "grizzled" appearance due to lighter tips on their guard hairs

3. **Body Structure**

   - Head: broad and concave facial profile (distinguishes them from black bears)
   - Shoulder hump: a prominent muscular hump used for digging and strength
   - Limbs: powerful legs with long, curved claws (2–4 inches) adapted for digging and handling prey

- Tail: short and inconspicuous, measuring about 3–5 inches (7.5–13 cm)
- Paws: large and wide, with a distinct, straight claw print (unlike the curved print of black bears)

4. Lifespan

- Wild: 20–30 years
- Captivity: up to 40 years

BEHAVIORAL CHARACTERISTICS

1. Activity

- Primarily crepuscular (active during dawn and dusk), but may be active day or night depending on human presence or food availability
- Hibernation:
  - Hibernate for 5–7 months in colder climates
  - During hibernation, heart rate slows to 8–12 beats per minute, and bears rely on fat reserves for energy

2. Diet

- **Omnivorous:** Brown bears have one of the most diverse diets among bears.
  - Plants: grasses, roots, berries, nuts, and fungi
  - Animals: fish (especially salmon), small

mammals, carrion, and occasionally large prey (e.g., moose or elk calves)

    ◦ Coastal bears rely heavily on salmon during spawning runs, which provide high-fat nutrition.

- Seasonal hyperphagia in late summer and fall leads them to consume up to 90 pounds (40 kg) of food daily to prepare for hibernation.

3. Social Behavior

- Solitary, except for females with cubs or during feeding aggregations (e.g., at salmon streams).
- Home ranges:
  - ◦ Females: 5–50 square miles
  - ◦ Males: 50–500 square miles

4. Communication

- Vocalizations: growls, roars, grunts, and huffs to signal aggression, contentment, or warning
- Body language: ear positioning, standing upright, and mock charges are common displays
- Marking: scratching trees, rubbing against objects, and leaving scent markings to establish territory

Adaptations

1. Digging Ability

- The shoulder hump provides exceptional strength for digging dens, unearthing roots, and hunting burrowing animals.

2. Swimming

- They are excellent swimmers, capable of crossing rivers and lakes in search of food.

3. Climbing

- They are less adept at climbing than black bears due to their size but can climb small trees when young or threatened.

4. Senses

- Smell: extraordinary sense of smell, capable of detecting food from miles away
- Hearing: acute hearing for detecting prey and potential threats
- Vision: good eyesight with color vision, aiding in foraging and identifying threats

Habitat

1. Range

- Found across North America, Europe, and Asia.

- In North America, populations are concentrated in Alaska, western Canada, and parts of the Rocky Mountains.

2. Preferred Environments

- They reside in coastal areas, forests, tundra, alpine meadows, and grasslands.
- Habitat selection depends on food availability and human disturbance.

3. Denning Sites

- Dens are typically dug into hillsides, beneath tree roots, or in caves to provide insulation and protection during hibernation.

REPRODUCTION

1. Mating Season

- Occurs from May to July.
- Males compete for females, and pairs may stay together for 1–2 weeks.

2. Gestation

- Delayed implantation: Fertilized eggs implant in the uterus in the fall, ensuring cubs are born during hibernation.

3. Birth

- Cubs are born in January or February.
- Litter size: 1–4 cubs (typically 2–3)
- Newborns weigh about 1 pound (0.5 kg) and are blind, hairless, and helpless.

4. Maternal Care

- Cubs stay with their mother for 2–3 years, learning survival skills like hunting and foraging.

Key Points About Brown Bear Birth During Hibernation

- **Hibernation Context:** Female brown bears enter a state of hibernation during the winter months. While hibernation, they are not in a true "deep sleep" but are in a state of reduced metabolic activity.
- **Birth:** The cubs are born during this period, typically while the mother is in her den. The birth process does not wake the mother completely from hibernation.
- **Cubs' Condition at Birth:** Cubs are born very small, weighing only about 1 to 1.5 pounds (0.5–0.7 kilograms). They are blind, hairless, and entirely dependent on their mother for warmth and nourishment.
- **Growth in the Den:** After birth, the cubs nurse on the mother's rich milk, which is high in fat, allowing them to grow rapidly. The mother does not eat, drink, or defecate

during this time, relying on her fat reserves to produce milk and sustain herself.

- **Emergence in Spring:** By the time the mother and cubs emerge from the den in the spring, the cubs are much larger, typically weighing around 10–15 pounds (4.5–7 kilograms), and are ready to follow their mother as she begins searching for food. This reproductive strategy allows the cubs to develop in the safety of the den while the mother conserves energy during the harsh winter months. Mothers are highly protective and will fiercely defend cubs from threats, including other bears.

AGGRESSION AND DEFENSE

1. **Aggression**
   - They generally avoid humans but can be highly aggressive when surprised, protecting cubs, or guarding food.
   - Defensive behaviors include mock charges, roaring, and standing on hind legs to intimidate.

2. **Predatory Behavior**
   - Rarely predatory toward humans but may stalk if food is scarce or they are habituated to humans.

THREATS

1. Natural Predators

- Adults have no natural predators, but cubs may fall prey to wolves, mountain lions, or adult male bears.

2. Human Interaction

- Habitat loss, hunting, and human-bear conflicts are the main threats.
- Improper food storage can lead to habituation, increasing the likelihood of conflict.

3. Conservation Status

- Classified as "Least Concern" globally, though some populations (e.g., grizzly bears in the lower 48 US states) are listed as threatened or endangered.

SUBSPECIES

1. Grizzly Bear (*Ursus arctos horribilis*)

- This inland subspecies is found in North America, smaller than coastal brown bears.
- Relies on a diet of plants, insects, and occasional large prey.

2. Kodiak Bear (*Ursus arctos middendorffi*)

- Found on the Kodiak Archipelago, Alaska.
- This is of the largest brown bear subspecies due to abundant salmon runs.

3. **Eurasian Brown Bear** (*Ursus arctos arctos*)

- Found in Europe and Asia, ranging from forests to alpine meadows.

Brown bears are remarkable creatures, symbolizing wilderness and resilience. Their adaptability and varied behaviors make them one of the most fascinating large carnivores in the world.

BLACK BEAR

PHYSICAL CHARACTERISTICS

1. **Size**

- **Length:** 4–7 feet (1.2–2.1 meters) from nose to tail
- **Height at shoulders:** 2.5–3 feet (0.7–0.9 meters) when on all fours; 5–7 feet (1.5–2.1 meters) while standing upright
- **Weight:**
    - Males (boars): 150–600 pounds (68–272 kg)
    - Females (sows): 90–300 pounds (41–136 kg)
    - Regional variation: Black bears in colder regions tend to be larger due to better food availability and longer hibernation needs.

2. **Coloration**

- Despite their name, black bears can be black, brown,

cinnamon, blond, or even white (e.g., Kermode or "spirit" bears in British Columbia).

- A white patch on their chest is common but not universal.

3. Body Structure

- Head: rounded ears and a straight facial profile, distinguishing them from grizzly bears, which have a concave profile.
- Limbs: strong legs with non-retractable claws, ideal for climbing trees and digging.
- Tail: short and stubby, measuring about 4–7 inches (10–18 cm).
- Paws: broad feet with sharp claws; front claws are shorter (1–2 inches) than those of grizzly bears, aiding in climbing.

4. Lifespan

- Wild: 10–20 years
- Captivity: up to 30 years

Behavioral Characteristics

1. Activity

- Diurnal and nocturnal: Primarily active during the day in less disturbed areas but can become nocturnal in human-populated regions to avoid encounters.

- Hibernation:
  - Black bears hibernate for 3–5 months in colder regions.
  - In warmer climates, some remain active year-round.
  - During hibernation, they do not eat, drink, urinate, or defecate, relying on fat stores.

2. **Diet**

- Omnivorous: consume both plant and animal matter
  - Plants: berries, nuts (acorns, beechnuts), grasses, and roots.
  - Insects: ants, bees, wasps, and larvae
  - Meat: carrion, fish, small mammals, and occasionally deer fawns.
- Seasonal hyperphagia in the fall drives bears to eat excessively to build fat reserves for hibernation.

3. **Social Behavior**

- Solitary animals, except for females with cubs or during mating season.
- **Home ranges:**
  - Females: 2–6 square miles
  - Males: 15–80 square miles

4. Communication

- Vocalizations: grunts, huffs, moans, and growls to signal contentment, agitation, or aggression
- Body language: Standing upright to appear larger, bluff charges, and ear positioning to express mood
- Marking: scratching trees and rubbing against objects to establish territory

ADAPTATIONS

1. Climbing Ability

- Excellent climbers due to strong, curved claws and powerful forelimbs
- Climbing used for foraging (e.g., nuts and fruits) and escaping predators

2. Swimming

- Strong swimmers capable of crossing lakes and rivers in search of food or new territories

3. Senses

- Smell: extraordinary sense of smell, approximately seven times better than a bloodhound's; used to locate food from miles away
- Hearing: acute hearing, allowing them to detect high-frequency sounds

- Vision: better than previously believed; color vision helps distinguish ripe fruits and detect movement

HABITAT

1. Range

- They are found across North America, from Alaska to Florida and northern Mexico.
- Their habitats include forests, swamps, mountains, and tundras.

2. Denning Sites

- Hollow trees, rock crevices, caves, or dug-out ground nests

REPRODUCTION

1. Mating Season

- Occurs between May and July.
- Males may travel long distances to find mates.

2. Gestation

- Delayed implantation: The fertilized egg remains dormant until fall, ensuring cubs are born during hibernation when the mother is safe and food is scarce outside.

3. Birth

- Cubs are born in January or February during hibernation.

- Litter size: 1–5 cubs (typically 2–3)
- Newborns are blind and hairless and weigh about eight ounces (227 grams).

4. Maternal Care

- Cubs stay with their mother for 1–2 years, learning survival skills such as foraging and climbing.
- Females are fiercely protective of their young, especially against males who may harm cubs.

AGGRESSION AND DEFENSE

1. Aggression

- They are generally shy and avoid humans unless provoked, surprised, or habituated to human food.
- Aggressive behaviors include bluff charges, jaw-popping, and growling.

2. Defensive Behavior

- Climbing trees or running away when threatened
- Defensive attacks are rare and typically occur to protect cubs

THREATS

1. Natural Predators

- Few predators, but cubs may be vulnerable to wolves, coyotes, or adult male bears.

2. Human Interaction

- Habitat loss, vehicle collisions, and hunting are major threats.
- Improper disposal of food and garbage can lead to bear habituation and conflicts.

3. Conservation Status

- Classified as "Least Concern" globally, though some local populations are declining due to human activity.

BEING IN BEAR COUNTRY

I was a bit nervous even though I had all the confidence in our guide, who was carrying a very large handgun strapped to his chest underneath his raincoat. But with this slight fear I was wondering: What if for some reason I was facing either a brown or black bear? What would I do, what should I do, and how should I react to defend myself?

BLACK BEAR (URSUS AMERICANUS)

GENERAL BEHAVIOR

- **Timid and Avoidant:** Black bears are generally shy and prefer to avoid confrontation.
- **Curious:** They may approach humans out of curiosity rather than aggression.

- **Less Likely to Defend Cubs:** Black bears are less protective of their cubs compared to brown bears and are more likely to flee.

DEFENSIVE STRATEGIES

1. **If the Bear Is Nearby but Not Aggressive:**
   - Stay calm and avoid eye contact.
   - Speak in a calm, firm voice to let the bear know you're human.
   - Slowly back away without turning your back.
   - Do not run—this may trigger a chase response.

2. **If the Bear Becomes Aggressive:**
   - Make yourself look larger by raising your arms or opening a jacket.
   - Use loud noises (shout, bang pots) to intimidate the bear.
   - Throw small objects (not food) in the bear's direction—not to hit it but to deter it.
   - If the bear attacks, fight back aggressively using anything at hand (sticks, rocks, fists). Aim for the bear's sensitive areas, such as the nose and eyes.

3. **Key Tip:**
   - Black bear attacks are usually defensive or predatory. Fighting back is typically effective because black bears will retreat if they perceive resistance.

Brown Bear (Ursus arctos, including grizzlies)

General Behavior

- **Defensive and Aggressive:** Brown bears are more likely to react aggressively, especially if surprised or defending food or cubs.
- **Highly Protective of Cubs:** Sows with cubs are particularly dangerous.
- **Territorial:** Brown bears are more likely to see humans as a threat when in close proximity.

Defensive Strategies

1. **If the Bear Is Nearby but Not Aggressive:**
   - Stay calm and avoid sudden movements.
   - Speak in a calm, low tone to signal you're not a threat.
   - Slowly back away, maintaining visual contact without staring directly at the bear.
   - Avoid running—this could trigger a chase.

2. **If the Bear Becomes Aggressive:**
   - Do not try to intimidate a brown bear by making yourself appear larger—this may provoke further aggression.
   - If the bear charges but stops short (a bluff charge):
     - Stand your ground and remain calm.

○ Do not move or retaliate unless the bear makes physical contact.

3. **If the Bear Attacks:**

- Play dead by lying flat on your stomach with your hands clasped over the back of your neck. Spread your legs slightly to make it harder for the bear to roll you over.

- Remain still until the bear leaves the area. Fighting back may escalate the attack.

- If the bear continues to attack and treats you as prey (rare for brown bears), fight back aggressively using any available object to target the eyes and face.

4. **Key Tip:**

- Brown bear attacks are often defensive. Playing dead can signal you're not a threat, causing the bear to lose interest.

SUMMARY OF DIFFERENCES

- **Black Bear Defense:** Be assertive, make noise, and fight back if attacked.

- **Brown Bear Defense:** Stay calm, play dead during a defensive attack, and only fight back if the attack is predatory.

PREPARATION TIPS FOR BOTH

- Carry and know how to use bear spray, which is highly effective for both species.

- Travel in groups and make noise while hiking to avoid surprising bears.

- Learn about bear behavior in the specific region you're visiting and avoid known bear feeding areas.

Understanding these differences can significantly increase your chances of surviving a bear encounter.

Shortly after, we entered a shallow area and began to spot a few sockeye salmon swimming below us. Dropping anchor, we grabbed our spinning rods and began flossing. Despite our efforts, we didn't catch a single salmon for the first hour. Finally, our luck changed—we flossed one.

The salmon fought wildly, leaping out of the water and splashing furiously as it tried to free itself. It arched its back and glistened in the sunlight as it thrashed against the water while hooked in the mouth. Each jump seemed a desperate attempt to escape, but he couldn't shake it free. As he neared the boat, we reached out with our net, captured him, and brought its squirming body onto the deck.

To end his suffering, we quickly struck it on the head with the bat. This was our practice. We thanked him for his life and made a little prayer to him to forgive us from taking his life and promised to honor him by not allowing his body to go to waste. Afterward, we moved to another spot on the river to try our luck again.

CHALLENGES OF FLOSSING SALMON

When flossing a salmon, you never know exactly where the hook will land. If it's hooked in the mouth, reeling it in is relatively easy. However, if the salmon is hooked elsewhere on its body, the process becomes much more challenging. As the fish is pulled perpendicular to the fishing pole, it encounters greater resistance due to moving through more water compared to when it's hooked in the head and swimming towards the boat.

In these cases, the effort feels more like dragging a weighted object than fishing. The horizontal pull increases the tension on the line in the water, making it feel significantly heavier and raising the likelihood of the hook slipping off its body.

We continued fishing, but the sockeye run did not seem to be in its full swing yet, and our catch was slow. About an hour later, our fortunes shifted when we caught a chum salmon instead of a sockeye. This was unexpected, as chum salmon were not yet migrating upriver—they were expected to arrive in one to two weeks. This particular chum must have been a stray.

SOCKEYE VS. CHUM SALMON

Sockeye salmon and chum salmon are two distinct species of Pacific salmon that differ in several key ways:

Sockeye salmon are renowned for their bright red to orange flesh and the vibrant red color they develop during spawning. They have a more streamlined body and a pronounced hook in the upper jaw, resembling a proboscis. Their entire body undergoes a remarkable metamorphosis, as they stop eating once they enter the river and begin their journey to the spawning grounds.

Chum salmon generally have a more muted coloration, with a greenish-blue back and silvery sides. During spawning, they develop distinct vertical stripes, and their bodies can become more bulbous.

Sockeye on dock

TASTE AND TEXTURE

- **Sockeye Salmon:** Highly regarded for its rich flavor and firm, fatty texture, sockeye is the most popular choice of salmon to eat.

- **Chum Salmon:** Considered less flavorful than sockeye, chum salmon has a milder taste and a softer texture. It is often used for canning and is prized for its roe (fish eggs).

HABITAT AND LIFE CYCLE

- **Sockeye Salmon:** Prefer cold, clean waters and are often found in lakes and rivers. They typically return to their natal streams to spawn, sometimes traveling long distances upstream.

- **Chum Salmon:** They are more adaptable to a variety of habitats, including coastal waters and rivers. Known for their extensive migrations, chum can spawn in a wider range of environments.

CULINARY USES

- **Sockeye Salmon:** Favored for its taste, it is commonly found fresh or frozen in markets. It is also widely used in sushi.
- **Chum Salmon:** Frequently used in processed products like canned salmon, with its roe considered a delicacy.

It's obvious why sockeye salmon are the preferred choice for most fishermen.

RETURNING TO THE LODGE

It was getting late, and we could tell Gavin was hungry and needed a break. At 11:30 a.m., we picked up the anchor and Gavin started the engine to head back to the lodge. As we approached, we noticed a large number of seagulls circling above the dock. Their presence was a clear sign that something was going on.

Birds are excellent indicators for fishermen, always on the lookout for fish. When seagulls or other birds dive into the water, it usually means fish are nearby—either as prey or feeding on smaller fish. There is an old adage among fishermen: follow the birds. Once spotted, you head toward the diving birds, slow the boat upon approach to avoid scaring the fish, and drop your lines.

Even bears along the Alagnak River use this strategy. When they see birds scavenging the riverbanks, the bears often follow this signal too, knowing that the presence of fish is not too far away. So, as we neared the dock and saw the flurry of activity, we knew something exciting awaited us.

Lauri caught the first Chum Salmon in the river, however when we got back to the lodge, we were all busy catching Sockeye Salmon. When I say we were all busy, nobody stayed behind at the lodge because everyone was there reeling in the fish.

A DOCK FULL OF FISH

To our delight, we found nearly everyone at the lodge—crew and guests alike—gathered on the dock with fishing poles in hand. Hundreds of sockeye salmon were swimming in the water beneath and around the dock. The excitement was palpable.

We jumped out of the boat, grabbed our rods, and joined the frenzy. Everyone was trying to floss the salmon, and the dock was scattered with nets ready to land the catch. By the evening, we all had success.

While we felt a twinge of sadness for the fish, we also knew their lives wouldn't be wasted. Every salmon caught was destined to be eaten, shared, and appreciated. Salmon are rich in omega-3 fatty acids, low in mercury, and delicious—a nutritious gift from the river.

I couldn't help but think of one of my patients who had recently turned 100 years old. When I asked her secret for the secret to longevity, she said, "I eat salmon a couple of times a week. No wheat, no sweet, and salmon as often as I can."

OMEGA-3 FATTY ACIDS

Omega-3s are essential fats with numerous health benefits:

1. Heart Health

- **Cholesterol Levels:** They help lower triglycerides and may raise HDL (good cholesterol).

- **Blood Pressure:** Linked to reduced blood pressure and overall cardiovascular health.
- **Inflammation Reduction:** Omega-3s have anti-inflammatory properties, reducing the risk of heart disease and stroke.

2. **Brain Health**

- **Cognitive Function:** Particularly DHA, omega-3s are crucial for maintaining brain cell structure and function.
- **Mental Health:** They may reduce symptoms of depression and anxiety and support mood stability.

3. **Eye Health**

- DHA is a major component of the retina, associated with a lower risk of age-related macular degeneration.

4. **Joint and Bone Health**

- **Anti-inflammatory:** Beneficial for conditions like rheumatoid arthritis.
- **Bone Health:** May improve bone strength and calcium absorption.

5. **Skin Health**

- Helps maintain hydration and elasticity, while improving conditions like psoriasis and eczema.

6. **Pregnancy and Infant Development**
   - Supports fetal brain and eye development and enhances breast milk nutrition.

7. **Metabolic Health**
   - Improves insulin sensitivity and supports weight management.

8. **Potential Cancer Prevention**
   - Some studies suggest protective effects against breast and colon cancer.

9. **Gut Health**
   - Reduces inflammation in the gastrointestinal tract, benefiting conditions like IBD.

10. **Longevity**
   - Associated with lower mortality rates from heart disease and other health issues.

Primary sources of omega-3s include fatty fish like salmon, mackerel, and sardines, as well as flaxseeds, chia seeds, and walnuts.

AN EVENING TO REMEMBER

The sockeye salmon we caught in Alaska provided us with the best nutrition the wilderness has to offer—a gift we didn't take for granted. Each trip to Alaska brings new experiences, but catching salmon always remains a highlight.

That evening, we enjoyed a wonderful meal at the lodge: freshly caught salmon served with rice, potatoes, salad, and dessert. After dinner, we were all exhausted from the day's excitement and turned in early, around 8 p.m., eager for the adventures the next day would bring.

With the commercial boats set to drop their nets again soon, I could only hope it wouldn't disrupt the salmon run upstream.

Lauri was well suited for her adventure. Those Grudens were quite the style here, as were the Grizzly bears foraging for food. They were in a fishing competition with us. Lauri caught the first sockeye salmon.

Chapter 6

July 17

Today, after breakfast, having caught plenty of sockeye salmon the day before, we left the dock with Gavin and headed north up the river for more fishing. About 10 minutes into the trip, we passed the same tall tree we had seen the day before. As expected, the American bald eagle was perched on its branch, scanning the river in search of prey.

Just like yesterday—what I now assume is part of its daily routine—the eagle stood in the exact same spot. But today, unlike yesterday, there were two eagles instead of one. They were perched close to each other, on two separate branches. Their piercing eyes seemed to scrutinize everything below them, searching for their next meal.

Their white heads and yellow beaks contrasted beautifully with their shiny brown feathers, which almost looked manicured in their neatness. About 100 feet away, on another tree branch, was a massive nest. Peeking out from the nest was a baby eagle, curiously watching us. I guessed that the two perched nearby were its parents, standing guard over their young while also hunting for breakfast.

Mother, Father and baby Eagles

Black Bear

Brown Bear

Eagle

I became fascinated by this family of eagles and wanted to learn more about them. What kind of eagles were they? In Alaska, two species of eagles are resident: the bald eagle and the golden eagle. I wanted to understand the differences between the two, so I did some research. Eagles usually live 20–30 years and, when mature, can weigh up to 14 pounds. Their speed during a hunting swoop can range from 30 to 90 mph—an astonishing feat of agility and power.

BALD EAGLE

1. Hatchling Stage

- **Color:** Hatchlings are covered in soft gray or white down feathers.
- **Timeframe:** This stage lasts about 5–6 weeks, during which they remain in the nest, developing strength and coordination.

2. Juvenile Stage

- **Color:** At around 5–6 weeks old, they begin growing dark brown feathers with mottled patterns. Their heads and tails remain dark.
- **Duration:** This stage lasts until they are about 3–4 months old, as they prepare to leave the nest.

3. Sub-adult Stage

- **Color:** From ages 1–4, they display a mix of dark brown feathers and the gradual emergence of white head and tail feathers. The transformation is slow and progressive.
- **Development:** By ages 4–5, they begin to achieve the distinct adult coloration.

4. Adult Stage

- **Color:** By the age of five, bald eagles reach full maturity, displaying their iconic plumage: a white head and tail with a dark brown body and wings.

I knew that being on the river, I would see many more eagles, but this first encounter with the family left a lasting impression. Witnessing their majestic natural habitat and learning about their life stages added a whole new level of appreciation for these incredible birds.

GOLDEN EAGLE

1. Hatchling Stage

- **Color:** Like bald eagles, golden eagle chicks hatch with soft, light gray down feathers. This stage lasts for the first few weeks.

2. Juvenile Stage

- **Color:** As they grow (around 5–6 weeks), their juvenile feathers develop, characterized by dark brown tones  with lighter streaks and a more mottled appearance. The head may show some golden feathers. This stage lasts until about one year of age.

3. Sub-adult Stage

- **Color:** From ages 1–4, they retain their dark brown feathers but begin developing more golden coloring on the back of the head and neck. Their wings may also develop white patches. The transition to full adult plumage is gradual, becoming more pronounced with time.

4. Adult Stage

- **Color:** By around 4–5 years old, golden eagles achieve their mature plumage. They exhibit a rich golden color on the head and neck, dark body feathers, and distinct white patches on the wings.

COMPARISON BETWEEN BALD AND GOLDEN EAGLES

- **Juvenile Feather Color:** Bald eagles are dark brown with mottling, while golden eagles are also dark but exhibit more streaks and hints of gold from an earlier age.
- **Adult Plumage:** Bald eagles are known for their stark white head and tail against a dark body, while golden eagles display a more uniform golden-brown appearance with highlights of gold.

Both species undergo significant changes as they mature, but their timelines and specific patterns reflect unique adaptations.

HUNTING SKILLS

Eagles are exceptional hunters, employing a variety of techniques and strategies to capture their prey. Here's what I learned about their hunting behavior:

1. **Vision**

    - **Exceptional Eyesight:** Eagles have incredibly sharp vision, allowing them to spot prey from distances up to two miles. Their eyes contain a high concentration of photoreceptor cells and a special membrane that enhances contrast.

    - **Depth Perception:** Their forward-facing eyes provide excellent depth perception, critical for judging distances during dives.

2. **Hunting Techniques**

    - **Soaring and Gliding:** Eagles use thermal currents to soar high above the ground, scanning for movement. This energy-efficient method allows them to cover vast areas.

    - **Perch and Pounce:** Often, eagles hunt from high perches like tree branches or rocky outcrops. From these vantage points, they swoop down with precision.

    - **Diving (Stooping):** Eagles can dive at speeds of up to 90 mph to catch prey by surprise. This technique is especially effective for birds and small mammals.

- **Stealth Approaches:** Eagles sometimes approach prey quietly, using cover to get closer before launching their attack.

3. **Prey Preferences**

   - **Diet:** Eagles are opportunistic hunters. Common prey includes fish, birds, small mammals like rabbits and squirrels, and even carrion.

   - **Specialization:** Bald eagles are excellent fishers and often hunt near water, while golden eagles focus more on terrestrial mammals.

4. **Group Hunting**

   - **Social Behavior:** Although typically solitary, some eagles hunt cooperatively when targeting larger prey. For example, they may work together to flush prey from cover.

   - **Territorial Defense:** Eagles are territorial and vigorously defend their hunting grounds, often engaging in aerial displays or aggressive interactions.

5. **Adaptations and Learning**

   - **Learning:** Young eagles learn hunting techniques from their parents, practicing by making attempts at catching prey until their skills improve.

   - **Adaptability:** Eagles adjust their strategies based on prey availability and environmental conditions, showcasing remarkable adaptability.

Sloughs of the Alagnak River

The Alagnak River has numerous sloughs, which serve critical ecological and functional roles:

1. **Definition:** A slough is a side channel or offshoot of the main river. It's often shallow and slow-moving, providing unique habitats.

2. **Formation:** Sloughs develop through sediment deposition, erosion, or flooding, creating a network of wetland-like areas adjacent to the river.

3. **Vegetation:** They support diverse aquatic and riparian vegetation, offering breeding and feeding grounds for various wildlife species.

Functions of Sloughs

- **Habitat:** Sloughs are havens for fish, birds, amphibians, and other wildlife, offering shelter and food resources.

- **Water Quality:** They help filter pollutants and sediments, improving the river system's overall health.

- **Flood Control:** Sloughs absorb excess water during floods, reducing strain on the main river channel.

- **Recreation:** These areas are excellent for fishing, birdwatching, and kayaking.

ENCOUNTERING A MOOSE

As we navigated through a few narrow sloughs, searching for fish, we rounded a bend and came upon a female moose standing at the riverbank, no more than 50 feet away. The

sheer size of her was astonishing—majestic yet imposing. She stood still, watching us with calm curiosity, her massive frame blending seamlessly with the dense vegetation around her. Moments like these remind me of the profound connection between the Alagnak River and the incredible wildlife that depends on it.

The male and female moose exhibit distinct differences in appearance and behavior.

APPEARANCE

MALE MOOSE (BULLS)

- **Antlers:** Males are known for their large, palmate (broad and flat) antlers, which can span up to six feet in width. These antlers are shed and regrown annually.
- **Size:** Bulls are larger than females, weighing 800–1,600 pounds and standing about 5–6.5 feet tall at the shoulder.
- **Body Features:** Males have a more robust and muscular build, with a pronounced neck and shoulder area. Their coats are often darker, a rich brown.

FEMALE MOOSE (COWS)

- **No Antlers:** Females lack antlers, a primary distinguishing feature. They have a more graceful head and neck compared to bulls.
- **Size:** Cows are smaller, weighing 500–1,100 pounds and standing about 4.5–6 feet tall at the shoulder.
- **Body Features:** Females have a sleeker body with a narrower appearance. Their coat is often lighter brown or tan, and their facial structure is more pronounced.

BEHAVIORAL CHARACTERISTICS

MALE MOOSE (BULLS)

- **Aggressiveness:** Bulls can be territorial, especially during the fall breeding season (rut). They may engage in dominance displays or fights with other males to secure breeding rights.

- **Mating Calls:** During mating season, bulls make loud grunts or bellows to attract females and assert their presence.

- **Solitary Nature:** Outside the rut, bulls are typically solitary, preferring to roam alone.

FEMALE MOOSE (COWS)

- **Maternal Behavior:** Cows are known for strong maternal instincts. They give birth to one or two calves (usually one) after an 8-month gestation period and will fiercely protect their young.

- **Social Structure:** Cows may form small groups, especially with calves. They are more social than males and often associate with other females and their offspring.

- **Feeding Habits:** Cows spend more time foraging in varied habitats, including wetlands and forests, to support their calves.

WHEN MIGHT A MOOSE ACT AGGRESSIVELY TOWARD HUMANS?

While moose, especially males, are not typically aggressive toward humans, certain circumstances can provoke defensive or aggressive behavior:

1. **Breeding Season Rut Behavior:** During the rut in fall, male moose become territorial and aggressive as they compete for mates. If they perceive a human as a threat, they may react aggressively.

2. **Protecting Calves**

   - **Maternal Defense:** While female moose primarily defend calves, a male may perceive a nearby cow and her calves as a reason to be defensive.

3. **Surprise Encounters**

   - **Close Proximity:** Moose can be startled by sudden movements or unexpected encounters, leading to defensive responses.

   - **Habituation:** Moose accustomed to human presence may feel cornered or threatened if approached unexpectedly.

4. **Injury or Illness**

   - **Stress or Pain:** An injured or sick moose may exhibit aggression as a defense mechanism.

5. **Food Scarcity**
   - **Irritability:** In areas with scarce food, moose may become more defensive or irritable.

6. **Seasonal Stress**
   - **Winter Conditions:** Limited food availability and harsh conditions during winter can lead to stress and increased aggression.

While moose attacks on humans are rare, maintaining a safe distance, especially during the rut or around calves, is crucial. If you encounter a moose, back away slowly and give it space.

OUR MOOSE ENCOUNTER

As we slowed the boat to a crawl, I realized we were facing a female moose, as she lacked antlers. She stood at the riverbank, seemingly startled by our presence, pausing to stare at us as we stared back at her. After a few moments, she turned her back and walked up the bank, disappearing into the sage and brush. We were in awe, yet relieved, as we weren't looking for a confrontation. It was a mesmerizing experience, locking eyes with this magnificent creature.

SIGNS OF SOCKEYE SALMON DETERIORATION

As we continued fishing, we observed some sockeye salmon swimming in the distance, their bodies showing clear signs of deterioration. Their skin had ulcerations, and they swam unbalanced, moving slowly and seemingly void of energy. Surprisingly, they didn't react to the noise of our boat engine or voices, likely due to their exhaustion.

Seeing these salmon in their natural process of decay was both fascinating and sad. It's incredible to think about how they sacrifice everything, even their lives, to ensure the survival of their offspring. This act of selflessness—dying to give life—is called semelparity.

SPECIES OTHER THAN PACIFIC SALMON THAT EXHIBIT SEMELPARITY

1. **American Eels**
   - These eels migrate thousands of miles to spawn in the Sargasso Sea, dying after expending all their energy.

2. **Mayflies**
   - Adult mayflies live only a day or two, during which they mate, lay eggs, and die.

3. **Cuttlefish**
   - Some female cuttlefish die shortly after laying eggs, having exhausted their energy reserves.

4. **Certain Spiders**
   - In species like black widows, males sacrifice themselves during mating.

5. Agave Plants

- After years of growth, the agave flowers dies, having dedicated all its resources to seed production.

BEAVER DAMS ALONG THE ALAGNAK RIVER

As we traveled farther upstream, we passed numerous beaver dams along the riverbanks. These structures play a vital role in the ecosystem:

- **Biodiversity:** Beaver dams enhance habitat diversity, providing homes for various aquatic and terrestrial species.
- **Water Quality:** They filter sediment and pollutants, improving the river's overall health.
- **Flood Control:** By slowing water flow, beaver dams help reduce flooding downstream.

Beaver Dam

While beaver dams can pose challenges to human activities, their ecological benefits make them invaluable to maintaining a

balanced environment.

Beaver dams are remarkable structures built by beavers that play a significant role in maintaining the health of the Alagnak River ecosystem. The construction, care, and maintenance of these dams are fascinating feats of engineering and have far-reaching ecological impacts.

1. Construction of Beaver Dams

- **Materials Used:** Beavers primarily use wood, branches, twigs, and mud to construct their dams. They may also incorporate stones and other natural materials when available.

- **Building Process:**
  - **Site Selection:** Beavers choose locations where water flow can be easily managed, often in streams, rivers, or wetlands.
  - **Cutting Trees:** With their strong teeth, beavers cut trees and gather materials efficiently.
  - **Dam Design:** Typically wedge-shaped, the dams have a broader base and taper upward. Heights can vary, ranging from a few inches to over 10 feet, depending on the landscape and the beavers' needs.
  - **Water Management:** By blocking the flow of water, beavers create a pond that protects their

lodge (a shelter structure) from predators and provides a stable water source year-round.

2. **Types of Dams**

- **Flat Dams:** Built across streams, creating wide, flat ponds.

- **Levee Dams:** Constructed along riverbanks to stabilize water levels.

3. **Ecological Impact**

- **Habitat Creation:** Beaver dams create wetlands, essential for supporting diverse species, including fish, amphibians, birds, and aquatic plants.

- **Water Quality:** These ponds filter sediments and pollutants, enhancing overall water quality.

- **Flood Control:** By slowing water flow, beaver dams reduce downstream flooding and recharge groundwater reserves.

- **Biodiversity Support:** Wetlands formed by dams are among the most productive ecosystems, fostering a rich variety of plant and animal life.

4. **Beaver Behavior and Lifestyle**

- **Social Structure:** Beavers typically live in family units, which include a breeding pair and their offspring. They work together to maintain their dam and lodge.

- **Lodges:** Beavers construct lodges using the same materials as their dams. These structures provide shelter and protect them from predators, often built in the center of the pond for added security.

5. **Impact on Human Activities**

- **Flooding:** Beaver dams can occasionally cause flooding in agricultural areas or along roadways, leading to conflicts with landowners.

- **Habitat Enhancement:** Conversely, these dams improve local ecosystems and offer recreational opportunities such as fishing and wildlife observation.

- **Management:** Various methods, including flow devices, help regulate water levels while allowing beavers to remain in their habitat.

6. **Beaver Dams and Climate Change**

- **Resilience:** Beaver dams help mitigate climate change effects by maintaining water levels during droughts and reducing flood impacts.

- **Carbon Sequestration:** Wetlands created by dams store carbon, aiding efforts to combat climate change.

7. **Cultural Significance**

- **Historical Importance:** Beavers were historically vital to Indigenous peoples and early settlers for their fur and their role in shaping landscapes.

- **Symbol of Conservation:** As a keystone species, beavers are integral to conservation efforts due to their ability to modify and sustain habitats.

I had never seen a beaver dam in person before, and it's incredible to imagine how an animal as small as a beaver can construct such a complex and functional structure.

A River Rich in Natural Beauty

The Alagnak River is not just about its animals and birds; it's also home to stunning vegetation that thrives in its challenging environment. During my first days on the river, I noticed clusters of beautiful pink and purple-blue flowers, along with patches of white blossoms that reminded me of boneset, snakeroot, and Queen Anne's lace from back home.

I hoped we'd find time to stop along the riverbanks to explore these plants more closely. Their beauty captured my attention, and I couldn't resist snapping pictures between fishing sessions.

Spruce Trees and Tide Effects

As 5:30 p.m. approached, we began our journey back to the lodge. Driving south, we noticed numerous spruce trees growing sideways along the muddy banks. Their roots, partially dislodged by erosion, caused them to lean almost horizontally. Yet, remarkably, they were still alive and thriving.

Upon arriving at the lodge, the steepness of the embankment stood out, exaggerated by the low tide. As we stepped onto the dock and over the gunnel of the boat, we spotted an Alaskan fox in the distance. This fox was quite different from the gray fox that lives under our deck in Fort Lauderdale, Florida.

Our gray fox at home is easily recognizable by its silver-gray coat with a reddish hue on the legs and chest, white belly and neck, and a long, bushy tail with a black tip and stripe. She has lived under our deck for years, raising her young there. We've come to admire her daily routine of emerging in the quiet mornings and evenings to forage or bask in the sun. She is sensitive to noise and avoids contact, yet we've coexisted peacefully, respecting each other's space.

In contrast, the fox we saw in Alaska appeared to be a red fox, distinguished by its reddish-brown coat with white interspersed throughout. Its coloring seemed perfectly adapted to this environment, perhaps aiding in camouflage against the snowy landscape during Alaska's long winters. Red foxes are known for their excellent sense of smell, sight, and hearing, which make them skilled hunters. This particular fox, though stunning, was cautious and quickly ran up the riverbank when noticed by us. It had likely been foraging for fish carcasses discarded into the river from the cleaning tables at the lodge.

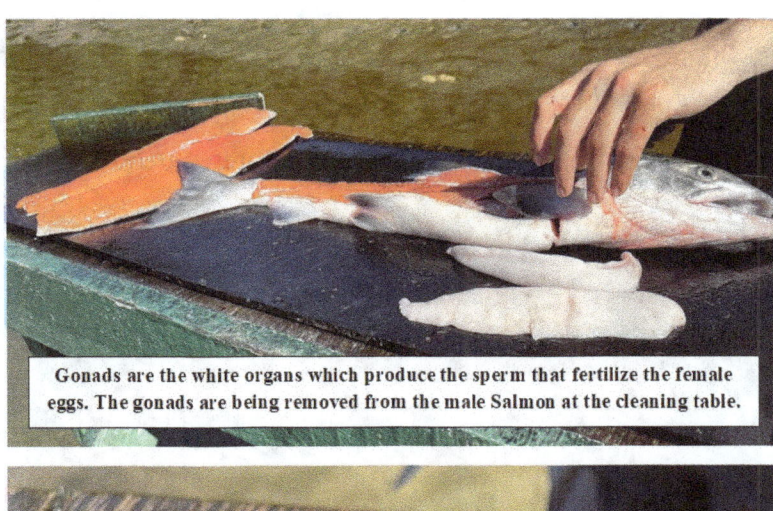

Gonads are the white organs which produce the sperm that fertilize the female eggs. The gonads are being removed from the male Salmon at the cleaning table.

The mouth of the Salmon became angulated looking like a proboscis. The gums are receded and thinning. The gums and tongue have turned dark grey in color. This is one of the signs of deterioration seen in a tired Salmon that has entered the river before dying.

As we approached the cleaning tables, we saw the Germans and some of the guides filleting their catch. They appeared satisfied with their successful day. We noticed them carefully saving the roe, or fish eggs, which piqued my curiosity. Initially, I thought they might use the roe as bait, as I had done during past fishing trips for king salmon. However, Glenn, their guide, reminded them that using bait is prohibited by law on the Alagnak River. All fishing here is done with lures, hooks, and artificial flies to preserve the ecosystem.

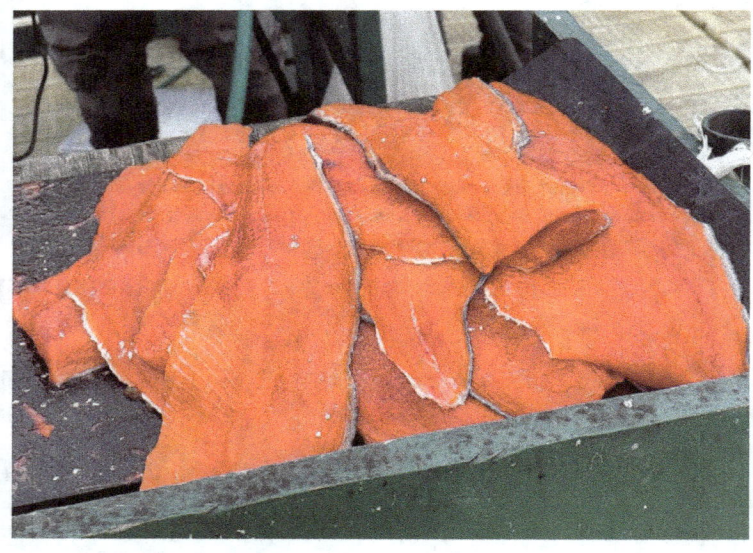

Instead, the Germans explained they planned to make caviar from the roe. While true caviar is traditionally made from sturgeon eggs, their process would create an imitation version using salmon roe. They described the basic technique of soaking the roe in a saline solution to break down the outer membrane and separate the eggs. This salt-curing process mimics how traditional caviar is made, creating a delicacy that we could enjoy later.

As we discussed the merits of caviar, movement on the riverbank caught our attention. A large brown bear was making his way down the slope toward the water, likely drawn by the scent of the fish that had remained floating downstream. Much like the fox earlier, the bear seemed intent on gathering his share of the bounty. After scanning the area and noticing us, the bear climbed back up the hill and disappeared into the wilderness. It was the second brown bear we had seen that day; earlier, another one had approached the lodge near our dining room window, but I'd missed the chance to photograph it. This time, I managed to capture a video of the bear as it descended the slope.

As the evening wore on, we tied our boat to the dock, leaving our gear behind, and climbed the famous 48 steps to the lodge perched atop the hill. Exhaustion hit me hard. My body was still adjusting to Alaska time, and after dinner I knew I wouldn't last long before heading to bed. The combination of fishing, observing nature, and soaking in the excitement of the day left me thoroughly drained each evening. Yet, as I drifted off to sleep, I couldn't help but feel anticipation for the adventures that the next day would bring.

CHAPTER 7

JULY 18

For the past five days since landing in Anchorage, the weather had been cloudy, rainy, and cold. Today, however, we were greeted with sunshine and a bright sky with fewer clouds. The temperature was forecasted to rise into the low 60s—a welcomed change from the 40s and 50s we had endured. Even with the river's vegetation providing some protection, the wind generated by the boat's speed added to the chill, making this pleasant weather in mid-July a bit nippy.

As I came down the steps from the second floor into the dining room, I noticed the delights of food awaiting us for breakfast: eggs benedict served on an English muffin, topped with chunks of freshly caught sockeye salmon and finished with a sprinkle of salmon roe—caviar prepared by our German friends. Kudos to them for the creative touch!

I picked up the eggs benedict and cautiously placed them in my mouth, letting my tongue explore the texture of the salmon caviar. As the roe rolled across my tongue, their consistency and flavor sent a delightful message to my brain. I couldn't help but smile. The salty pop of the eggs, combined with the rich salmon and creamy hollandaise, was an exciting experience. I devoured the rest of this concotion with my voracious appetite. The roe was slightly saltier than I preferred; I thought that if I prepared caviar myself, I'd rinse it more thoroughly to temper the saltiness. A touch of hot sauce made the taste perfect, and I pursued the meal until it was totally gone.

After breakfast, I completed my daily ritual of swallowing my 25 nutraceuticals with three handfuls of water. What a phenomenal start to the day!

Out on the River

Today's weather was slightly better than the previous days, but still cold and cloudy, with temperatures lingering in the 40s and 50s. Layered in my warmest clothing, I was prepared for the chill that came while cruising at 30–40 mph on the boat. Gavin pulled the line on the Yamaha engine, and with the roar of the engines behind us, we sped off into the crisp morning air.

I wore two head caps under a Grundéns yellow resin of a synthetic hoodie, and my body was wrapped in layers: two T-shirts, a long-sleeved shirt, a thick wool jacket, and the Grundéns all-weather windbreaker. For my lower half, I wore underwear, long johns, heavy camel-hair pants, and Grundéns waterproof black overalls secured with straps. These layers were essential to ward off the wind's icy bite as the boat glided swiftly over the water.

As Gavin drove, I examined the fishing hooks he had prepared for the day. Some were adorned with feathers, while others featured spinning jigs. Gavin, now in his third season on the Alagnak, was extremely knowledgeable and carried himself with confidence and a calm demeanor that made fishing with him a pleasure.

FISHING AND EXPLORATION

Fishing was slow today. The commercial boats at the river's mouth had dropped their nets, halting much of the salmon's migration upstream. We saw only a few fish, and many were already in a state of decay. Gavin decided to take us through the river's sloughs—narrow channels cutting through the riverbanks. These sloughs, lined with sage and grasses, were beautiful and peaceful.

I've developed a growing appreciation for wild vegetation in recent years. At home, I collect photos of wild and invasive plants, sometimes arranging samples in vases to highlight their beauty. Seeing the vibrant greenery along the Alagnak River rekindled my interest, and I couldn't wait to explore the riverbanks more closely.

VEGETATION ZONES IN ALASKA

Alaska's diverse topography and climate create distinct vegetation zones or biomes, each characterized by unique plant communities adapted to their environments:

- **Low and Mid-Elevations (Coastal Plains):** These areas, with their temperate climate, often support rainforests.

- **Mid-Elevations (Boreal Forests):** Known as taiga, these forests are dominated by coniferous trees like the spruce, pine, and fir. Boreal forests are the largest land biome on Earth, stretching across northern North America, Europe, and Asia.

- **High Elevations (Alpine Tundra):** At higher altitudes, the landscape transitions to alpine tundra, where only hardy grasses, shrubs, and mosses can survive.

The Alagnak River sits within the boreal forest zone, and its vibrant plant life reflects this biome's resilience. I found myself captivated by the banks' natural beauty—splashes of pink, purple, blue, white, yellow, and green blending harmoniously. The tall grasses and sage lining the river seemed perfectly manicured, as if nature itself had orchestrated a masterpiece.

RETURNING TO THE LODGE

As the day wore on and we caught no fish, we returned to the lodge. Passing through the sloughs and marveling at the vegetation had been a satisfying alternative to fishing, but it left us eager for better luck tomorrow. I could not wait to take some time off our fishing day to explore the sides of the riverbanks, to get a closer view for identification. I could see all sorts of colors in these plants, varying from pink to purple, blue, white, yellow, and green. Wow, that's the kind of stuff that is so stimulating to my eyes. It just captivates me. The tall grass, reeds, and sage that line the banks of the river seemed as if they were planted by God, so well manicured by nature's own creation. Harmonious they were, moving with the stroke of the wind, all in one direction, inspiring a feeling of a well-rehearsed concert.

When we returned to the lodge, Robert had prepared a hearty dinner of brisket with mashed potatoes. The meal was comforting and delicious, a perfect end to the day. Exhausted, I headed upstairs to bed, with a body that was still struggling to adjust to the Alaskan time zone. The excitement and effort of each day left me drained, but I couldn't wait to see what adventures tomorrow would bring.

A dilapidated historic remanent of a village that used to exist along the edge of the river.

Northern upper part of the Alagnak River

CHAPTER 8

JULY 19

Breakfast began at 7 a.m., featuring freshly made eggs and salmon tacos. With a dash of hot sauce and salmon caviar, the meal was delicious. Unfortunately, the coffee was still without its Sweet'N Low, a disappointment I was still adjusting to.

As we left the lodge and headed toward the 48 steps leading to the river, we passed several spruce trees along the walkway. Just before the stairs, to our right, stood a willow bush adorned with fluffy, feather-like growths that danced in the wind, releasing seeds that floated like snowflakes. Once we stepped into the boat and

headed down the river, I noticed an abundance of these seed tufts drifting through the air and landing on the water.

WILLOW BUSHES AND SEED DISPERSAL

Willow bushes (*Salix* species) are common along rivers and wetlands in Alaska, including the Alagnak River. Their seeds are attached to fluffy white structures called "coma," which disperse when the wind blows. Willows bushes typically release their seeds in late spring to early summer, but some species can continue into July, depending on the local climate. The sight of these seeds dispersing was like snowflakes, enchanting and beautiful, adding to the serene atmosphere.

The weather remained cloudy and overcast, but thankfully stayed dry. We buttoned up to keep warm as we ventured onto the river.

ANOTHER ENCOUNTER WITH A BROWN BEAR

A short way upriver, we encountered another brown bear. Its color and size suggested that it was not the same one we had seen earlier. This bear was crossing the river, and as we tried to get closer for a better view, it quickened its pace to escape us, disappearing into the brush.

Like the previous day, the fishing was slow. The commercial fishing boats at the river's mouth were again permitted to deploy their nets, catching thousands of pounds of salmon while sport fishermen like us were left struggling and hanging.

THE CONFLICT BETWEEN SPORT AND COMMERCIAL FISHERMEN

The tension between sport and commercial fishermen in Alaska over salmon fishing has deep roots and reflects economic, environmental, and cultural complexities.

EARLY HISTORY

- **Indigenous Practices:** For thousands of years, Native Alaskans have relied on salmon for their sustenance, culture, and economy.
- **Commercial Expansion:** The late 19th and early 20th centuries saw a boom in commercial fishing with the advent of canning technology and increased settlement.

POST-WWII GROWTH

- **Technological Advances:** The postwar era brought rapid growth in the commercial salmon industry, boosting both the economy and fish processing industries.
- **Regulation Begins:** Overfishing concerns led to the introduction of seasons, bag limits, and designated fishing areas.

1970s–1990s

- **Sport Fishing Advocacy:** Anglers began pushing for stricter regulations to protect salmon populations. Sport fishing organizations emerged to advocate for conservation and fairer resource allocation.

- **Litigation:** Court battles ensued over fishing rights, leading to management strategies designed to balance the interests of both sectors.

MODERN DEVELOPMENTS

- **Regulatory Adjustments:** Emergency closures and other measures aim to protect salmon spawning runs while balancing economic needs.

- **Environmental Focus:** Broader concerns about climate change, habitat destruction, and sustainable practices have shaped ongoing debates.

This ongoing struggle reflects a complex interplay of tradition, economics, and conservation, with both groups striving to ensure the sustainability of Alaska's salmon populations.

TURNING TO TROUT

With salmon scarce due to commercial netting, we turned our attention to trout fishing. Alaska mandates the release of all trout caught in certain rivers to support conservation efforts and maintain ecological balance. These rules ensure healthy trout populations for future generations.

Lauri, as usual, caught the first trout—a beautiful greenish-silver specimen. After taking pictures, we carefully released it back into the river.

TROUT IN ALASKA

Alaska is home to three primary types of trout: lake trout, rainbow trout, and cutthroat trout. Among these, rainbow trout are especially popular due to their vibrant colors and spirited resistance when caught, making them a favorite among anglers.

Rainbow Trout

Rainbow trout are a popular freshwater fish known for their vibrant colors and fighting spirit, making them a favorite among anglers. Here's a detailed description:

Courtesy of Rainbow Trout USFNS National Digital Library

Physical Characteristics

- **Coloration:** Rainbow trout have a distinctive appearance with a dark green to grayish-brown back, often speckled with light spots (vermiculations) and a lighter belly. Their fins are typically translucent with white edges.
- **Size:** They are among the largest freshwater fish, with adults typically ranging from 5 to 30 pounds, though some individuals can exceed 50 pounds in ideal conditions.
- **Body Shape:** Rainbow trout have a long, streamlined body with a deeply forked tail, adapted for life in deep, cold waters.

HABITAT

- **Distribution:** Native to North America, rainbow trout are predominantly found in Canada, the northern United States, and Alaska. They have also been introduced to other regions worldwide.

- **Environment:** Preferring cold, oxygen-rich water, rainbow trout are commonly found in deep lakes with rocky or gravelly bottoms. During the summer, they often inhabit depths of 50–200 feet, following the cooler temperatures.

BEHAVIOR AND DIET

- **Diet:** Rainbow trout are apex predators in their ecosystems, feeding on smaller fish, crustaceans, and aquatic insects. In some lakes, they may primarily prey on species like cisco or smelt.

- **Spawning:** They spawn in the fall, typically over rocky shoals or gravel beds in shallow areas of lakes. Unlike rainbow trout, lake trout do not construct nests (redds) but instead scatter their eggs, leaving them to develop without parental care.

RECREATIONAL IMPORTANCE

- **Popularity:** Rainbow trout are a prized species for

recreational anglers due to their size, strength, and the challenge they present. Ice fishing for rainbow trout is particularly popular in northern regions.

- **Stocking:** Many lakes are stocked with rainbow trout to support sport fishing and maintain ecological balance in waters where native populations may be struggling.

CONSERVATION

- **Threats:** Habitat destruction, pollution, and competition with non-native species, such as invasive lake trout in Yellowstone Lake, pose significant challenges. Overfishing has also historically impacted certain populations.
- **Management:** Conservation efforts focus on habitat restoration, controlling invasive species, and implementing fishing regulations to ensure sustainable populations.

LAKE TROUT

Lake trout are a keystone species in many freshwater ecosystems and a valuable resource for recreational fishing. Their role as both predator and prey contributes to the ecological balance of the aquatic habitats they inhabit.

Physical Characteristics

- **Coloration:** Lake trout have a distinctive coloration with a dark green or grayish back, lighter sides, and a pale, almost white belly. Their sides are often adorned with light-colored spots, which can vary in size.

- **Size:** They can grow quite large, typically reaching weights of 10–30 pounds, though some individuals can exceed 40 pounds.

- **Body Shape:** Lake trout have a streamlined, elongated body with a broad head and a deeply forked tail.

Habitat

- **Distribution:** Lake trout are primarily found in deep, cold, and clear lakes. They prefer areas with abundant oxygen, often inhabiting deeper waters during warmer months.

- **Environment:** These fish are typically associated with

rocky substrates and underwater structures, which provide shelter and hunting grounds.

BEHAVIOR AND DIET

- **Diet:** Lake trout are carnivorous and primarily feed on other fish, including smaller species like cisco and whitefish, as well as aquatic insects and invertebrates.
- **Spawning:** They usually spawn in the fall, using rocky areas in shallow water to lay eggs. Lake trout are known to have a longer lifespan, with some individuals living over 30 years.

RECREATIONAL IMPORTANCE

Lake trout are popular among anglers due to their size and the challenge they present when caught. They are often targeted in both summer and winter fishing, particularly in northern regions where ice fishing is common.

CONSERVATION

Lake trout are a species of freshwater fish native to North America, particularly found in the cold, deep lakes of Canada and the northern United States. While lake trout populations can be stable in many areas, they face threats from habitat degradation, overfishing, and competition with invasive species. Conservation efforts focus on managing fishing practices and protecting habitats to ensure the sustainability of lake trout populations.

Lake trout are a significant species in freshwater ecosystems and are prized by both recreational fishermen and conservationists for their ecological and economic value.

CUTTHROAT TROUT

Cutthroat trout are a native North American species known for their distinctive coloration and adaptability to various environments. Here's a detailed overview:

PHYSICAL CHARACTERISTICS OF CUTTHROAT TROUT

- **Coloration:** Cutthroat trout display vibrant coloration, with a greenish or olive back, yellowish sides, and a white belly. Their most distinguishing feature is the red or orange slash marks on their throats, giving them their name.

- **Size:** Typically ranging from 1 to5 pounds, cutthroat trout can grow larger in optimal conditions.
- **Body Shape:** These trout have a streamlined body, a pointed snout, and a slightly forked tail, perfect for their active lifestyle.

Habitat

- **Distribution:** Found across western North America, cutthroat trout inhabit a variety of habitats, including streams, rivers, and lakes, especially in mountainous regions.
- **Environment:** They thrive in cold, clear, oxygen-rich waters and can adapt to both freshwater and saltwater environments.

Behavior and Diet

- **Diet:** Opportunistic feeders, cutthroat trout consume insects, crustaceans, small fish, and other aquatic organisms. Their diet varies depending on habitat and food availability.
- **Spawning:** Spawning typically occurs in spring, with females laying eggs in gravel beds in streams and rivers.

SUBSPECIES

Cutthroat trout include several subspecies, such as:

YELLOWSTONE CUTTHROAT

Known for its yellowish coloration and found in the Yellowstone region.

- **Coastal Cutthroat:** Often inhabits estuarine environments along the Pacific coast.
- **Lahontan Cutthroat:** A larger subspecies native to the Great Basin.

RECREATIONAL IMPORTANCE

Cutthroat trout are prized by anglers for their striking appearance and the challenge they provide. They are a popular target in both freshwater fishing and catch-and-release programs.

CONSERVATION

While many populations are stable, some subspecies face threats from habitat loss, competition with non-native species, and overfishing. Conservation efforts emphasize habitat protection and population management to ensure sustainability.

Cutthroat trout are an iconic species, celebrated for their beauty, adaptability, and importance in both ecosystems and recreational fishing.

Reflection and Exploration

The slow fishing day gave us time to admire the riverbanks, dotted with sage and tall grasses that seemed meticulously manicured by nature. I marveled at the wild vegetation, vibrant in hues of pink, purple, blue, white, yellow, and green—a palette that felt like a divine masterpiece. I couldn't wait to take a closer look at these plants during our trip, as their beauty was captivating and inspired my growing interest in flora.

The Rest of the Day on the Alagnak River

At 11:30 a.m., we started heading back to the lodge for a quick bite to eat. About an hour and a half later, we returned to the river. The cloudy sky was beginning to break apart, revealing glimpses of beautiful blue hues. By early afternoon, the sun's rays were streaming through, warming us up as the day progressed.

Despite the better weather, our fishing efforts remained fruitless for most of the day. It seemed likely that the sockeye salmon run had concluded. Even if it wasn't over, the commercial fishing boats at the river's mouth were blocking any substantial movement of fish upstream.

Although the fishing wasn't productive, we continued to enjoy the breathtaking scenery, observing the wildlife and the lush vegetation that lined the riverbanks. Being out on the river, even without catching fish, was a satisfying reminder of Alaska's untouched beauty.

Rami is chilling out on the Alagnak River, fishing for Salmon.

THE ALAGNAK RIVER'S HISTORY AND SIGNIFICANCE

As we navigated the Alagnak River and its sloughs, we passed abandoned homes along its banks, some standing for over a century. These remnants sparked reflections on the region's history and the resilience of its native inhabitants.

HISTORICAL INSIGHTS

- **Early Settlements:** The Alagnak River has been a lifeline for humans for thousands of years, supporting prehistoric settlements, fishing camps, and trading outposts.

- **Cultural Legacy:** Evidence of historic villages remains, including an old Russian Orthodox church and cemetery along its banks.

- **Challenges of Survival:** Harsh winters with heavy snow and sub-zero temperatures posed significant challenges to those living here, underscoring their ingenuity and perseverance.

THE MEANING OF "ALAGNAK"

The name "Alagnak" comes from the Yup'ik word meaning "making mistakes." It reflects the river's ever-shifting channels and maze-like sloughs, which can easily confuse or disorient travelers. Locals often call it the "Branch River," a nod to its constantly changing pathways. The Yup'ik pronunciation is "Ah-lock-anok."

A DAY OF EXPLORATION

As we ventured through the Alagnak's sloughs, we marveled at the rich biodiversity and historical significance of this river. Though fishing was slow, the experience of witnessing the river's natural beauty, its complex network of channels, and the cultural history etched along its banks was a profound reminder of Alaska's rugged allure.

PREHISTORIC PEOPLE ALONG THE ALAGNAK

The human history of the Alagnak Wild River is a fascinating narrative woven from the combined efforts of Native residents, archaeologists, historians, and ethnographers. This story began over 14,000 years ago, after the last Ice Age, when glacial ice receded, allowing plants, animals, and early Americans to colonize the pristine landscape. While we may never know the identity, language, or belief systems of the first humans to set foot here, archaeological evidence reveals glimpses of their lives through the remains of camps and artifacts.

TIMELINE OF HUMAN PRESENCE ALONG THE ALAGNAK RIVER

- **12,000 BP:** Glacial ice from the last Ice Age retreated from the Alagnak River drainage, leaving a landscape ready for colonization.

- **9,000 BP:** Evidence of human occupation appears along riverbanks and lake outlets, with campsites near the headwaters dating back as far as 9,000 years.

- **2,500 BP:** Pottery, made from local clay and tempered with hair, down, sand, or gravel, became common. These artifacts reflect a more settled lifestyle and a growing dependence on the river's resources.

- **2,200 BP:** Most archaeological village sites along the Alagnak date to this period. A reconstructed ceramic vessel from site DIL-161, flat-bottomed and 7.5 inches high, is approximately 2,100 years old.

TRADITIONAL LIFESTYLE ALONG THE ALAGNAK (150 YEARS AGO)

The Alagnak River corridor was actively inhabited during the Little Ice Age, which ended about 150 years ago. Camps and villages dotted the riverbanks, sustaining life through the time of contact with Russian traders and missionaries. Until the late 19th century, the Alagnak was home to the Alutiiq and Central Yup'ik peoples, who lived in close-knit, kinship-based communities.

Seasonal activities defined life along the river:

- **Spring:** hunting beluga whales in Bristol Bay and gathering bird eggs, sour dock, wild celery, and fiddlehead.
- **Summer:** fishing for salmon to smoke, dry, and freeze for winter.
- **Fall:** harvesting salmonberries, crowberries, and blueberries; moose, caribou, and bear.

Salmonberries   Crowberries   Fiddlehead Ferns

Caribou   Wild Celery   Grayling   Sea Otter   Mink

Courtesy of US LIFE Service and Alaska Fishing Goods

- **Winter:** ice fishing for smelt, trout, and grayling; trapping fur-bearing animals like mink, otter, and fox for clothing or trade.

Transportation was essential for survival. Kayaks served as primary transport during warmer months, while sled dogs became indispensable during the frozen winters.

20TH CENTURY CHANGES

By the early 20th century, the rise of canneries and commercial fishing transformed the region. Cash from the salmon industry allowed subsistence users to purchase store-bought goods like coffee, tea, and salt. Historically, villages like "Sleepy Town" and others along the Alagnak, Nonvianuk, and Branch River were populated with semi-subterranean and above-ground log houses. However, by the 1960s and '70s, these settlements were abandoned as families moved to nearby communities like Levelock, Igiugig, Kokhanok, and Naknek, drawn by modern opportunities.

Banana Cream Pie
and Chocolate Pudding Pie were
beyond delicious and were all
prepared by Chef Robert.

RETURNING TO THE LODGE

Around 5:30 pm, we headed back to the lodge for dinner. The Germans had caught a few chum salmon and were visibly pleased with their success. Dinner was another hearty and satisfying meal, and we retired for the night. Adjusting to Alaska's long daylight hours remained a challenge for me. With the sun not setting until around 11 p.m., I struggled to fall asleep, as my body was still in

New Jersey's time zone, four hours ahead. By 8 p.m. here, it felt like midnight back home, and I found myself exhausted by the day's activities. Waking up at 6 a.m. was manageable, as it felt like 10 a.m. in New Jersey. But the days here were long and physically demanding. For now, I remained in a jet-lagged haze, trying to acclimate to this new rhythm of life along the Alagnak.

CHAPTER 9

JULY 20

Today followed the same familiar routine: up at 6 a.m., layered in warm clothing, and heading to the dining hall to join the rest of the group for breakfast. After finishing, we made our way out and down the 48 steps (steps in my mind that inadvertently represent the lower 48 states, with Alaska being the 49th state). While this interpretation is my own, maybe they do represent the number of states that are associated with our lower 48 or maybe it's all just fortuitous. I couldn't help but think this every time we used them.

Once at the dock, we climbed into our flat-hulled johnboat with its 40-horsepower Yamaha engine. Gavin, our guide, started the motor and off we went, following the same rhythm we had been perfecting over the last few days. This routine was becoming second nature, as though we had done it a thousand times before. I was wrapped up in my usual four layers of clothes on my upper body and three on my lower body. Ready for the day.

Morning on the River

We headed north, upriver, away from the mouth, which was about five miles south of us. As we passed familiar sights, we saw the bald eagles perched in their usual spots. The two of them, likely a mated pair, stood vigil on the same tree branches as on previous days, scanning the river and banks for breakfast. Their juvenile offspring waited in the background, partially hidden by the thick foliage now. He was out of the nest.

Unlike its parents, the young eagle lacked the distinctive white head and tail feathers that bald eagles are known for. Instead, its feathers were dark brown, with only a few white ones scattered here and there—a camouflage that helps juveniles blend into their surroundings. They won't develop the iconic adult plumage until they are 4–5 years old. In the meantime, they rely on scavenging dead fish or other easy prey while they learn to hunt. Eagles are opportunistic feeders, always conserving energy while securing food, needing only about 0.6–1 pound of food a day, or roughly 450–550 calories. Their sharp vision, 20/5 compared to our 20/20, allows them to spot prey from incredible distances, a vital adaptation for survival.

EXPLORING AND FISHING

We drove past old, abandoned villages along the banks of the river, their lopsided, decaying walls teetering precariously close to the water. It seemed only a matter of time before the remnants collapsed entirely. These buildings, long deserted, served as quiet reminders of the history of this place.

We stopped at various spots, casting both spinning rods and eight-weight fly rods, but nothing was biting. After trying different areas, we shifted to fishing for trout, but even they eluded us. Despite the lack of success, the serene river and beautiful surroundings made it worth every moment.

As I sat in the swivel chair on the boat's deck, rhythmically casting my line, the mosquitoes began their relentless assault. Despite my layers and liberal use of repellent, they still managed to find ways to bite. I wasn't sure if it was real or just my imagination, but either way, I didn't like it. Yet, even with the minor annoyances, I felt lucky to be here, soaking in the stunning views under the warm sun, which had brought the temperature up into the 60s. Time slipped away as the hours passed in peaceful contentment.

EVENING AT THE LODGE

At 5:30 p.m., we decided to head back to the lodge for dinner. Tonight was bittersweet, as it was our last evening with the Germans. Bruno and his son were leaving in the morning on the small Cessna 206 floatplane. Before parting ways, we said our goodbyes and thanked Bruno for sharing his knowledge of making salmon caviar with us.

After another satisfying meal, I was exhausted. The time difference still had me out of sync. New Jersey is four hours ahead, so even though it was only 8 p.m. here on the Alagnak, my body felt like it was midnight. By the time my head hit the pillow, I was fast asleep, ready to repeat another day of adventure tomorrow.

CHAPTER 10

JULY 21

This morning, we bid farewell to our German friends as they departed for their floatplane. After saying our goodbyes, Gavin approached us with a proposal: to tour the northern part of the Alagnak River. He explained that heading toward Katmai Lodge would offer us a completely different perspective of the river and its surroundings. Although it was quite a journey and would take most of the morning, we decided to go for it. Fishing hadn't been fruitful over the past two days, so exploring seemed like the next best option.

Gavin's enthusiasm and genuine desire to ensure we had the best experience influenced our decision. He was a great guide—authentic, kind, and knowledgeable. When I agreed to the trip, he nodded with a big smile. We were geared up, between our layering of clothes and our Grundéns windproof and waterproof clothing, we were prepared for the chilly morning temperatures in the low

50s. After ensuring everything was securely stowed in the boat, we set off upriver.

A Journey Up the Alagnak

As we sped along at 35–40 mph, the wind still was able to cut through our layers, making the ride brisk despite the clear, sunny sky. The river twisted and turned, flanked by banks lined with tall grasses and sage that seemed meticulously arranged, as if painted into the landscape. Behind the grasses, dense forests of spruce trees created a natural wall so thick it was impossible to see beyond them. Nature's perfection was on full display.

Further upriver, the scenery began to change. The trees gave way to tundra—an unexpected sight. This nearly treeless landscape was marked by low grasses and shrubs, a stark contrast to the lush greenery we had passed earlier. The tundra's barren appearance was a testament to the harshness of the environment, where conditions were too extreme for trees to survive. The riverbanks were shallower here than further south down the river. This was likely due to erosion. The mountains loomed faintly in the distance. The lack of vegetation and muted tones of the tundra gave this area a different kind of worldly feel.

Gavin had been right: This journey was essential for us to fully understand the full character of the Alagnak. The river's subdued current in this section explained why salmon traveled so far upstream. In these calmer waters, they could dig gravel pits called redds near the banks to lay their eggs. Here, the salmon could spawn undisturbed, and their fertilized eggs would hatch into alevins and then fry. These young salmon would remain in the river for several years, undergoing the smolting process to adapt to the saltwater environment before heading to the ocean. Seeing this part of the river underscored the incredible life cycle of these fish.

Approaching Katmai Lodge

As we neared Katmai Lodge, Gavin slowed the boat. On our left, a cluster of brown wooden buildings stood near a fuel dock. Several boats, similar to ours, were tied there. Katmai Lodge has been a fixture on the river for over a century, founded around 1922. During our week of fishing, we often saw their boats passing us, along with others from Anglers Alibi, another lodge upriver. Katmai Lodge, however, was much farther up the river—around 20 miles north of our lodge. When we saw boats coming down the river toward our lodge, having traveled so many miles to fish in our area instead of staying closer to their own lodge, it reaffirmed our decision to choose the Alagnak Lodge, as it was clearly the better location for fishing. We were glad we had not chosen to stay at the Katmai lodge; the daily commute to our better fishing spot which is where we were fishing near the mouth of the river ,would have made the commute exhausting.

As Gavin navigated us past the lodge, we unexpectedly ran aground. The river was shallow here, and Gavin hadn't realized how tricky this section would be. He quickly jumped out to push the boat off the sandbar, apologizing profusely. His sincerity and determination to give us a memorable experience were evident, and we reassured him there was no need to apologize. Gavin's effort to show us this part of the river was appreciated, and we admired his honesty and dedication.

HEADING BACK

On the return trip, Gavin picked up speed, eager to get us back to the lodge in time for lunch. As we docked at 12:30 p.m., we heard someone calling Gavin's name in a frantic tone. "Gavin! Gavin!" they shouted repeatedly. Gavin bolted off the boat, running up the 48 steps to the lodge. His urgency was palpable, and we knew something was wrong.

Feeling uneasy, Lauri and I got out of the boat to stretch and prepare for whatever might unfold. Minutes passed like hours as we waited, unsure of the situation. When Gavin returned, he seemed nervous, his demeanor noticeably different. It took some coaxing, but eventually, he shared the story.

THE INCIDENT AT THE LODGE

Robert, the chef, had been drinking heavily the night before and that morning. His intoxication had led to a violent outburst in the dining room, where he threatened to kill one of the guides. Wade, a 350-pound former football player, had tackled Robert to the ground when he charged the guide, Mat. With the help of Gavin and others, they restrained Robert, zip-tying his hands and feet to prevent further harm. Although Robert didn't have a weapon, the threat alone was enough to alarm everyone, especially given his access to firearms.

The police were called, but being stationed in King Salmon, they couldn't arrive for several hours. In the meantime, the team moved Robert to an upstairs bedroom to wait for the authorities. However, while locked in the room, Robert started a small fire, likely in a desperate attempt to escape. Glen and Wade quickly extinguished the flames and decided to move Robert outside, tying him to a tree to prevent further chaos.

REFLECTING ON THE CHALLENGES

By the time the police arrived and took Robert away, those in the lodge were visibly shaken. We appreciated the staff's efforts to shield us from the drama, and we reassured Tony, the lodge owner, that we understood. Events like these, while rare, highlight the unique challenges of operating remote lodges in Alaska. Recruiting and retaining staff in such isolated locations is no easy feat, and occasional incidents are almost inevitable.

Despite the day's disruptions, dinner was delicious—more salmon, expertly prepared even without Robert. We couldn't help but feel a mix of sadness and relief. Sadness for Robert, whose struggles with alcohol had led him to this, and relief that the situation had been resolved without further harm.

Alaska's beauty and isolation come with inherent difficulties, but these challenges make places like Alagnak Lodge all the more real and remarkable. It's a testament to the resilience and dedication of those who work tirelessly to maintain these incredible off-the-grid experiences for guests like us.

CHAPTER 11

JULY 22

It was our last day on the river, and Gavin asked what we truly wanted to do. Knowing the river's fish population had dwindled and that we'd had no luck fishing over the past three days, I expressed my desire to explore and learn more about the vegetation along the banks. Taking photos of the plants that thrived in this unique ecosystem was something I was genuinely excited about. We decided to dedicate the time between breakfast and lunch to exploring the riverbanks.

Docking along the banks, we prepared to step off the boat. The hull gently brushed against the reeds and tall grass as we disembarked onto the muddy, gravel-laden ground. Climbing up the slope, we were greeted by a tapestry of wildflowers and plants, whose vibrant colors and intricate shapes captured our full attention. I eagerly began snapping pictures, hoping to identify each species later

Gavin, the guide

Our first discovery was a plant called **white burnet**. It resembled a stalk of wheat, standing tall on a slender stem. Its feathery, white petals hung loosely and seemed to shimmer in the daylight. When touched—or even stirred by the faintest breeze—its petals released a delicate, snow-like fuzz that floated through the air. It was mesmerizing to watch.

Though I had hoped to use my iPhone for the plant identification app, I quickly remembered that there was no internet in this remote wilderness. That didn't deter us; the beauty and mystery of these plants made the experience even more special. We carefully collected cuttings, photographing each one before placing it in a small bag for preservation.

The morning was filled with moments of discovery, an appreciation for the raw, unspoiled nature of the Alagnak River, and a sense of awe for the resilience of these plants in such a challenging environment. It was the perfect way to spend our final hours on the river, blending exploration, learning, and a deep connection to this remarkable place.

Flowers of the Alagnak

Next, we came across a striking **purple-blue iris**, its delicate petals standing tall and proud along the bank. Carefully, we cut the flower at the lowest part of its stem, envisioning a bouquet filled with the beauty of this wilderness. The vibrant hues of the iris contrasted beautifully with the greenery surrounding it, making it a centerpiece in our growing collection.

As we continued, we noticed a cluster of plants with white, tightly convoluted flowers that seemed familiar. After a closer look, we realized it was **yarrow**, a plant reminiscent of the ones we often see back home in New Jersey. Its feathery leaves and dense flower clusters added a delicate texture to our collection, blending beautifully with the iris and white burnet.

Each discovery felt like a small triumph, a connection between this remote Alaskan environment and the flora we knew from other parts of the world. With every new plant we identified, we felt more in tune with the rich and diverse tapestry of life along the Alagnak River.

However, the plant that stood out the most was **fireweed**—a stunning perennial with vibrant pink flowers arranged symmetrically around the stem. Each flower displayed four broad, light-pink petals, with smaller, darker pink petals nestled between them, creating a striking contrast. Inside this delicate arrangement were slender stigmata, adding a touch of elegance to the already beautiful blooms.

Clusters of fireweeds blanketed the field where we stood, painting the landscape with a gorgeous pink hue. It was mesmerizing to see how these hardy plants thrived in this rugged environment, their vivid colors contrasting brilliantly against the greenery and the muted tones of the surrounding wilderness. This breathtaking display of fireweed was undoubtedly the highlight of our botanical exploration along the Alagnak River.

The fireweed initially struck me as invasive due to its ubiquity along the riverbanks and fields. For days, it seemed to appear everywhere, leading me to wonder if it should be the flower representing Alaska. However, I later learned that the state flower is the **alpine forget-me-not**, and my assumption about fireweed being invasive was incorrect. In reality, fireweed is an iconic and highly valued plant in Alaska.

Common throughout south-central and southeast Alaska, fireweed is celebrated for its vibrant purple petals and its versatility. Alaskans use fireweed to make honey, jelly, and tea, and the plant is also edible. Remarkably, it's nontoxic to cats, dogs, and horses. One of fireweed's most significant ecological roles is its ability to pioneer disturbed or damaged areas, making it a key player in repairing ecosystems and preventing soil degradation and erosion. Its resilience and usefulness make it a true symbol of the Alaskan landscape.

Another striking plant we observed along the riverbanks was the towering **cow parsnip.** This plant, with its thick, hollow stems and cauliflower-like flower clusters, is as ubiquitous in Alaska as some of the invasive species in New Jersey. Cow parsnip, though large and prevalent, is not an invasive species in Alaska. It is native to North America and thrives in the Pacific Northwest and Alaska.

However, unlike fireweed, caution is necessary when handling Cow's Parsnip. Its sap can cause a photosensitive reaction on the skin, potentially leading to a rash. We were careful to avoid contact with the sap when we snipped the stems.

Cow parsnip is prolific across south-central and eastern

Alaska, evoking comparisons to some of our plants back home by its appearance, such as snakeroot, Queen Anne's lace, and boneset. Despite its abundance, the towering presence of cow parsnip adds to the unique charm of Alaska's wild flora.

The similarities between the plants we encountered in Alaska and those we know about from New Jersey are remarkable, even though they go by different names in each region there are so many similarities. We are all connected by six degrees. Along the banks, we also saw an abundance of ferns, which added to the lush and diverse vegetation.

The time flew by as we wandered along the riverbanks, exploring and photographing the local flora—a pastime Lauri and I both love. Before we knew it, it was time to head back to the lodge for lunch. Frankly, neither of us needed to eat, but we went mainly for Gavin's sake. He was eager for a hearty meal and the camaraderie of sharing stories with the other guides, who always had fascinating tales to tell about their morning adventures on the river.

At the lodge, meals and outings were organized into sessions: morning, afternoon, and evening. We usually chose the morning and afternoon sessions because we were often too tired for the evening ones. But since it was our last day, Gavin generously invited us to join him for a rare third session. We were still holding out hope for the chum salmon—or "dogs," as the guides often called them—to begin their run into the river. Although we were exhausted, we couldn't bring ourselves to decline. We knew it was our last night, and we appreciated Gavin's thoughtful invitation. These quiet, reflective rides had become special to us, and we enjoyed our conversations with him. Therefore, when dinner was over we left the lodge and got into the johnboat. Despite our efforts, the fishing was as unproductive as it had been for the past three days. We cast our spinning rods and fly rods tirelessly along the shallow banks, but not a single bite rewarded our persistence. The occasional sight of eagles soaring overhead, or perched regally on their usual branches, provided moments of distraction and wonder.

By 8 p.m., we conceded defeat and joined Gavin for one final outing to watch the sunset on the river.

During our outing, Gavin confided that the hardest part of his job as a guide was managing the long stretches of boredom and monotony while remaining focused. He also admitted that saying goodbye to people he had grown fond of was always challenging. I often wondered how a bright, mature 22-year-old like Gavin coped with the isolation and lack of social experiences that many young people his age could not do without.

It takes a particular kind of person to thrive in such a remote, off-the-grid environment. The job requires a deep love and passion for nature, coupled with discipline, resilience, and a strong sense of commitment. Gavin embodied all these qualities, which is why he returned for three consecutive seasons. I admired his perseverance and dedication, traits that not everyone possesses. He deserved all the respect and credit for what he had accomplished.

As we meandered through the river and its sloughs, the low sun bathed the landscape with its golden light, casting long shadows and filtering through the tree branches. The gentle breeze against our faces and the tranquil sounds of nature lulled us into a peaceful state. By 9 p.m., we began our journey back to the lodge. As we reached the docks, the quietness suggested that everyone else had already retired.

That night, as we drifted off to sleep, we reflected on the bittersweet realization that the next day would be our last in this beautiful, remote wilderness. Just as we were beginning to acclimate being off the grid and embracing the serenity of this untouched world, it was time to leave. It felt almost too soon to say goodbye.

CHAPTER 12

JULY 23

The day had finally arrived for us to leave the Alagnak Lodge and River. It was bittersweet—leaving one incredible experience to embark on another adventure. Over the past days, I had grown to admire the crew, getting to know their lives and appreciating their hard work. They were good-hearted people, and we shared a deep connection through our mutual love for nature, waters, fishing, and the wilderness. I expressed my gratitude to Tony Behm multiple times for the lodge and his team. Without Tony's vision, determination, and effort, the Alagnak Lodge wouldn't exist, nor would we have had our unforgettable experiences. The crew's dedication, passion, and skills were just as integral to the lodge's magic.

Still, I couldn't help but feel sorry for what had happened to Robert. I hope he will find his way back and overcome his struggles with drinking.

From left to right Rami, Lauri, Gavin, Peter, Glen, Tony Bohm, Tony, Mat and Owen behind

Our bags were packed, and the guides carried them down from the second floor to the makeshift elevator, which lowered them down the embankment to the dock. The staff then walked the bags to the floatplane waiting on the river. As I stood by, I marveled at the sheer volume of luggage and boxes, wondering how it would all fit into the small Cessna 206. It amazed me that such a small plane could handle this load and still take off safely.

The plane arrived on time, around 9 a.m., and the crew gathered on the dock for a group photo before we departed. Flying back to King Salmon in the Cessna 206 was, as always, a mix of thrill and unease for me. These small planes always leave me a bit on edge with their single engine and low altitude. I sat in the back seat, recording the journey on my iPhone, hoping that one day I might get used to these flights.

We arrived in King Salmon with three suitcases, three carry-ons, and three boxes of freshly caught sockeye salmon. Knowing we had enough fish to last us for a year or two brought immense satisfaction. I've always preferred catching my own fish—there's something reassuring about knowing exactly where it came from, how it was handled, and how quickly it was frozen. There's simply no comparison to the rich, nutrient-packed flavor of fresh red Pacific sockeye salmon.

After passing security, we waited outside, next to the tarmac for a few minutes before being allowed to board the Alaska airplane Boing 737-800/900. The plane took off on time and landed at Anchorage 45 minutes later. It was a sunny, clear day and the flight was very calm. When we landed at the Anchorage airport, we had to find a freezer that would store our boxes of frozen fillets from the Alagnak. We would leave them here at Anchorage until our return in about ten days from Homer with a fresh catch of other fish. From Anchorage, now with the fish from the Alagnak and Homer, they would eventually be shipped to Newark, New Jersey. Therefore upon landing at Anchorage we asked some employees at the terminal where the frozen storage was kept and based on their suggestion we walked with our boxes on an airport cart towards that area. Unfortunately, here is where we had our first bad experience in Alaska. After paying the clerk we met at the door, he took $75 to hold our fish boxes for each day they would be there. I thought that it was too much but felt that we had no choice. After we left, and while walking through the airport, we found another retailer who was located in the city of Anchorage called AK Trophy. We spoke to Nick, the owner, who agreed with us and said that he would store our catch for a lot less money. He was a super nice man on the phone and seemed very accommodating. Nick was not only more affordable but had gained my trust almost immediately. He agreed to pick up our boxes from the airport, store them for two weeks while we fished in Homer, and later combine our catch to ship them all together to Newark, New Jersey.

We discussed our plan with him and explained to him that we would be fishing in Homer for the next two weeks. We devised a plan for him to pick up our additional boxes when we got back to Anchorage from Homer with our halibut and then everything would be sent home the next day to Newark. It all seemed too good to be true, and even though I had some apprehension, I took a leap of faith, as we all sometimes do. I mean, Nick could have disappeared with our boxes of sockeye salmon, for all I knew. We had a lot of fish and I guess there was no telling for sure that they would all be there when we arrived home, but like I said, we decided to commit to the leap of faith and to Nick

Nick's professionalism and transparency gave us confidence, so we felt somewhat comfortable and decided to move our fish out of the airport's freezer to his facility.

When we returned to the airport freezer to retrieve our boxes, which was no more than 30 minutes, this is what happened: The same attendant who had taken our money insisted on charging us for a full day of storage. His stubbornness and lack of flexibility were frustrating, and we had no choice but to pay the $75. Not even a discount for the mere 30 minutes that they were held in their freezer. It was an unfortunate experience, but we quickly put it behind us and transferred our boxes to Nick, who promptly arrived at our hotel and reassured us about the shipping process.

After leaving the Anchorage airport we checked into the Alex Hotel and decided to grab a late meal at the nearby Lakefront Hotel, home to the Fancy Moose Lounge. The restaurant's unique attraction was its proximity to a lake where floatplanes landed and took off right over people's dining tables. People would sit there, order their meal, and watch the planes fly up and down on the lake. The planes were so close to our heads that you felt like you could touch them. Wow, how cool is that! So we sat down and ordered a couple of meals and watched the planes go up and down and heard their buzzing right above our heads. After doing this for a couple of hours as the evening wore on, fatigue set in, and we returned to the Alex Hotel. Tomorrow, we would fly to Homer for the next leg of our adventure. As I drifted to sleep, I reflected on the day—a mix of gratitude for the unforgettable experiences we'd had at the Alagnak Lodge and excitement for what lay ahead in Homer.

Chapter 13

July 24

Early the next morning, we made our way to the airport and boarded a DASH 8-100 twin-turboprop plane. Unlike the floatplanes we had used previously, this one was a regular small plane with wheels, which felt like a nice change. The flight to Homer from Anchorage took about an hour and was quite pleasant. Through the windows, we admired snow-capped mountains and distant glaciers.

Upon landing at Homer's small but clean airport, we noted its simplicity—it was even smaller than King Salmon's airport, without gift shops or other frills. The most prominent feature was the Pioneer Car Rental kiosk, where we picked up a small Ford SUV for our stay. It took us only about 15 minutes to drive to our Airbnb on Main Street. After unloading the vehicle, we headed to the town's main grocery store, Safeway, to stock up on supplies for the next nine days. We planned to fish for six or seven of those days, with our departure scheduled for August 3.

One reason we weren't fishing every day was that halibut fishing is prohibited on Wednesdays in Homer. This regulation, part of federal conservation efforts, helps manage halibut populations by reducing fishing pressure. It ensures sustainable practices and allows stocks to replenish. Despite my attempts to book an alternative trip for rockfish or other species on Wednesday, all the boats were fully booked months in advance. The fishing season in Homer is relatively short, starting in late May or early June and running through late August or early September. Even though fishing in New Jersey may offer a more diverse range of species throughout the year, with each season bringing unique opportunities to anglers, we do not have halibut, salmon, or rockfish there, the species they have in Alaska.

In New Jersey, fishing for the most part consists of the following:

SPRING (MARCH–MAY)

- **Striped Bass:** Begin their migration early in the spring, particularly in the warmer waters of southern New Jersey.

- **Winter Flounder:** Found in shallower waters, especially early in the season.

- **Bluefish:** Arrive toward late spring as water temperatures rise.

- **Black Drum:** Common in late spring, especially in Delaware Bay.

- **Tautog (Blackfish):** Inshore fishing for tautog is popular, though they move to deeper waters as temperatures rise.

SUMMER (JUNE–AUGUST)

- **Fluke (Summer Flounder):** A summer favorite, especially in bays, rivers, and nearshore reefs.

- **Weakfish (Sea Trout):** Often found in coastal bays and estuaries.

- **Sea Bass:** Peak season for sea bass along reefs and wrecks.

- **Mahi Mahi (Dolphin Fish):** Offshore anglers can target mahi mahi in warmer waters.

- **Bluefin and Yellowfin Tuna:** Popular targets for offshore anglers in mid-summer.

- **Sharks:** Shark fishing for species like sandbar, dusky, and thresher sharks peaks in summer.

FALL (SEPTEMBER–NOVEMBER)

- **Striped Bass:** The fall migration brings larger striped bass closer to shore, making this a prime season.

- **Bluefish:** Continue to be abundant until the water cools significantly.

- **False Albacore (Little Tunny):** Known for their speed and fight, they're common in late summer and fall.

- **Blackfish (Tautog):** Return inshore as temperatures cool, becoming a staple of fall fishing.

- **Sea Bass and Porgies:** Both species are commonly caught near rocky structures and wrecks.

WINTER (DECEMBER–FEBRUARY)

- **Blackfish (Tautog):** Winter is prime season for larger tautog, often caught near jetties, wrecks, and reefs.

- **Cod:** Found in deeper, colder offshore waters during winter months.

- **Ling (Red Hake):** A favorite among deep-sea anglers in winter.

- **Pollock:** Another popular deep-sea catch, often found alongside cod.

Each season offers unique opportunities, with spring and fall particularly favored for striped bass, while summer provides a broader variety of warm-water species. Winter is more challenging but can yield rewarding catches like tautog and cod.

WHY IS IT THAT THERE IS SO MUCH BIODIVERSITY WHEN COMPARING NEW JERSEY AND ALASKA FISHERIES?

The diversity of fish species off the coast of New Jersey compared to Alaska can be attributed to several ecological, geographical, and climatic factors:

1. **Biodiversity and Habitat Variety**

   - **New Jersey:** The Mid-Atlantic waters off New Jersey feature diverse habitats, including estuaries, tidal marshes, and artificial reefs. This variety supports a wide range of fish species, such as striped bass, bluefish, flounder, sharks, and tuna. Each habitat suits different life stages and behaviors of various species.

   - **Alaska:** Alaska boasts a rich marine ecosystem, with iconic species like salmon, halibut, and cod. However, its harsh environment and colder waters limit the variety of species. Fewer species are highly adapted to the cold, which reduces overall biodiversity compared to temperate regions like New Jersey.

2. **Temperature and Ocean Currents**

   - **New Jersey's Warm Waters:** Coastal waters are

influenced by the Gulf Stream, which brings warmer waters and supports a greater variety of fish species. These conditions enhance growth and reproduction among many species, contributing to high biodiversity.

- **Alaska's Cold Waters:** Alaska's nutrient-rich but frigid waters sustain specific species well-adapted to the cold, like salmon, pollock, cod, and halibut. However, the colder temperatures restrict the range of species that can thrive.

3. **Fishing Regulations and Practices**

- **New Jersey:** The fishing industry in New Jersey is diverse, with both recreational and commercial fishing targeting a wide array of species. This variety helps maintain the population and availability of multiple fish species.

- **Alaska:** Regulations in Alaska prioritize the sustainability of key species like salmon and halibut, creating a more focused approach to commercial and recreational fishing. This limits the range of species targeted compared to New Jersey.

In Summary

The broader variety of fish species in New Jersey is due to its temperate climate, diverse habitats, and influence from the Gulf Stream. Alaska, while abundant in its marine resources, is more specialized, focusing on species adapted to its colder, harsher environment. Each region offers unique fishing experiences, showcasing the distinct ecological advantages of their respective waters.

Since Homer's fishing season is shorter and boats book quickly, planning trips well in advance is crucial. While some fishing begins as early as April, the season truly kicks off in June when most boats are in the water.

In preparation for our first trip tomorrow, we decided to scout the Homer Spit to save time and avoid getting lost in the morning. The Homer Spit is a remarkable geographical landmark—a 4.5-mile-long strip of land extending into Kachemak Bay. It houses the Homer Boat Harbor, which accommodates up to 1,500 commercial and recreational boats at its summer peak.

Exploring the Spit, we located the next day's party boat and took some time to absorb the stunning surroundings. The narrow landform was bustling with activity—boats, shops, and restaurants all adding to its charm. We appreciated how practical it was to prepare ahead of time, knowing that any delays the next day could affect our fishing plans.

With everything set, we returned to our Airbnb and turned in early, excited for our first day of fishing on the pristine waters surrounding Homer.

Businesses on the Spit are mostly on the boardwalks.

Two different theories explain the origin of the Homer Spit.

One suggests it formed over millennia through the tidal swells and currents of Cook Inlet and Kachemak Bay, which gradually built up sand. The other theory attributes its creation to now-retreated glaciers that pushed the landmass into place. The Dena'ina people referred to the Spit as *Uzintun*, meaning "extends out into the distance." In 1899, the Cook Inlet Coal Fields Company constructed a railroad along the Spit, connecting docks to coalfields around Kachemak Bay. This development laid the foundation for the eventual establishment of Homer, Alaska.

At just 19 feet above sea level, the Homer Spit is vulnerable to storm surges, tsunamis (potentially triggered by nearby volcanic eruptions), climate change, and erosion. The ocean-facing side is especially exposed to heavy waves, presenting ongoing challenges.

As we left our Airbnb and turned left out of the driveway, we were immediately treated to an extraordinary view of the Kenai Mountains. The steep road we traveled offered a vantage point of Kachemak Bay set against the backdrop of those majestic peaks. The scene was a mesmerizing palette of greens, blues, and whites—breathtakingly gorgeous.

The sides of the road were dominated by massive cow parsnip plants growing wild and untamed, creating a striking, almost overwhelming display. Their sheer abundance was astonishing, carpeting the landscape with their towering presence. It was nearly impossible to keep my eyes on the road while surrounded by such beauty. These plants were thriving everywhere, from the roadside to the Homer Spit itself, lending a wild and vibrant character to the area.

We also spotted **curly dock weeds** along the way. Their tall, rough stems were adorned with leaves and clusters of curled, maroon-brown flowers, adding another layer of texture to the landscape. Even the weeds here had their own rugged charm, perfectly in tune with the untamed beauty of Homer.

Driving south along the Sterling Highway, also known as Alaska Route 1, we approached the Homer Spit. Before reaching the Spit's northern connection to the mainland, we passed a serene body of water on the east side of the road—Beluga Lake. The lake, named after the majestic Beluga whales, added to the picturesque charm of the journey. Here's some information about the fascinating marine mammals for which the lake was named after:

BELUGA WHALES: NATURE'S ARCTIC SINGERS

Beluga whales, often called "white whales," are remarkable for their unique adaptations, vocal abilities, and social behavior.

PHYSICAL CHARACTERISTICS

- **Color:** Belugas are born gray and gradually transition to white by the age of five. This white hue serves as camouflage in icy Arctic waters.

- **Size:** Medium-sized whales, they range from 13 to 20 feet in length and weigh 1,000–3,500 pounds, with males typically larger than females.

- **Distinctive Features:** Their rounded forehead, or "melon," is flexible and aids in sound production. They lack a dorsal fin, which allows for easier navigation under sea ice.

HABITAT AND RANGE

- **Arctic and Subarctic Waters:** Belugas thrive in the cold Arctic Ocean and surrounding seas, with some populations migrating seasonally and others remaining in Arctic waters year-round.

- **Global Presence:** Found primarily around North America (especially Alaska and Canada), Russia, and Greenland.

DIET AND DIVING ABILITIES

- **Diet:** Belugas are carnivorous, feeding on fish, crustaceans, and cephalopods like squid and octopus.

- **Diving Skills:** While capable of diving to depths of 2,000 feet, they usually forage in shallower waters. Their incredible flexibility allows them to hunt under tight ice formations.

SOCIAL BEHAVIOR

- **Highly Social:** Belugas form pods of 10–20 individuals, but during summer, they may congregate in the hundreds or thousands in shallow estuaries or coastal areas.

- **Vocalization:** Known as the "canaries of the sea," belugas produce a wide range of sounds—clicks, whistles, and chirps—for communication, navigation, and finding food. Their echolocation is highly advanced, aiding in Arctic navigation.

- **Curiosity:** Belugas are intelligent and inquisitive, often approaching boats or interacting with divers.

REPRODUCTION AND LIFESPAN

- **Mating and Birth:** Mating occurs in spring, and calves are born gray after a 14- to 15-month gestation period. The young nurse for about two years, staying close to their mothers.

- **Lifespan:** They can live 35–50 years in the wild.

CONSERVATION AND THREATS

- **Status:** Listed as "Near Threatened" by the IUCN, with some populations like the Cook Inlet belugas critically endangered due to pollution, habitat destruction, and climate change.
- **Threats:** Belugas face challenges from industrial activities, habitat encroachment, loss of sea ice, and pollution. In some regions, they are hunted for subsistence by indigenous communities.

FUN FACTS

- **Intelligence:** Belugas are known for their playful and intelligent behavior, often showing curiosity toward humans.
- **Mimicry:** Some belugas have displayed the ability to mimic human speech and sounds, highlighting their vocal flexibility.

As we drove past Beluga Lake, its tranquil waters seemed a fitting tribute to the majestic creature it was named after. The journey toward the Homer Spit continued to captivate us, both with its natural beauty and the fascinating stories tied to it. As we continued driving south on the Sterling Highway toward the Homer Spit, we passed Beluga Lake, where a collection of floatplanes were docked along its banks. Some planes appeared privately owned, while others belonged to the Homer Sea Planes Aviation Center, flying passengers to various destinations across the Kenai Peninsula. A bright red helicopter stationed near the lake immediately caught my eye.

Beluga Whale

Beyond the lake, the road was lined with clusters of commercial and retail businesses. These included the Homer Fish Processing Company, which we would use to vacuum-pack and flash-freeze our fish. The highway narrowed to two lanes—one heading north and the other south. As we continued south, the scenery transformed into a breathtaking panorama.

Ahead, the Homer Spit came into view, surrounded by the stunning backdrop of Kachemak Bay and the Kenai Mountains. The scene was so vivid and surreal that it nearly took my breath away. It felt as though I was driving into a living masterpiece. The Kenai Mountains appeared so close that I could almost reach out and touch them, though I knew they were miles away across the bay. To my right lay the northern side of Kachemak Bay, and to my left, the southern side. The sheer beauty of the view left me mesmerized.

This experience etched itself into my memory. The raw, unmatched beauty of the place made me realize I had made the right decision to visit Homer, Alaska. It was one of the most profound moments of my life, rivaled only by experiences in places like Iceland and Israel. I felt incredibly fortunate to be here, immersed in such natural splendor.

We soon located the Rainbow Tours sign, nestled among the many retail shops along the Spit. Inside, we met Kathy, who appeared to be in charge of the operation. She greeted us warmly and reviewed our itinerary for the next nine days. Having exclusively booked with Rainbow Tours, I was relieved that everything seemed well-organized. Kathy provided detailed information about the three boats we would be using. She exuded an air of confidence, suggesting she was well-versed in handling all the arrangements that we had made with Rainbow Tours. A small part of me had a twinge of apprehension—was it a mistake to put all my eggs in one basket?

Kathy reassured us, providing a detailed rundown of our itinerary. Over the next several days, we'd be on three different boats, each with its own unique schedule and crew. The *Spirit*, captained by Ross and supported by deckhands Patrick and Brice, would be our afternoon vessel. At 65 feet, the *Spirit* was built to accommodate up to 25 passengers and only went out for afternoon trips. She would turn out to be a reliable workhorse.

For only one full-day adventure, we were scheduled on the *Patriot*, a 30-foot aluminum boat captained by Drew, with Sam as his deckhand. The *Patriot* was a smaller, more intimate boat, designed to carry only six passengers. Outfitted with rod holders along its rails, it promised an efficient fishing experience. Inside was a single table with two bench seats, enough to seat four people. Another bench by the window could accommodate three more. Up front, the captain's chair stood by the wheel, and there was a small cuddy cabin at the bow, just big enough to fit a person or two. The *Patriot*'s trips started early at 7 a.m. and returned at 6 p.m., but the schedule often depended on whether the passengers caught their halibut limits early. The *Patriot* would be a longer trip and would venture farther offshore, increasing the chances of landing bigger fish.

The third boat in our lineup was the *Foxfire*, the morning counterpart to the *Spirit*. Slightly smaller than the *Spirit*, it carried fewer passengers but seemed no less capable. Captain Grant helmed the *Foxfire* with two crew members: James, a man in his late 30s who moonlighted as the owner of a dinner-only restaurant called the Canary in Homer, and Luke, a younger, less experienced deckhand who looked like he was in his twenties.

Kathy took her time guiding us through the logistics—where each boat was docked, which slips to find them in, and how to navigate the sprawling Homer Harbor. It was clear that her insight was invaluable; without it, we'd have spent the early hours of the morning scrambling to locate the right dock at the risk of missing our departure. The harbor itself was vast and intricate, a hub of activity that could easily overwhelm the unprepared.

Thanks to Kathy's thorough explanations, we left feeling more confident about the days ahead, ready to take on the adventures Rainbow Tours had in store for us. Kathy guided us through the layout of Homer Harbor, explaining where to find the slips and docks for each boat. The harbor was expansive, and without this prior reconnaissance, we might have struggled to locate the right spots in the early morning. This preparation ensured we could begin our fishing adventures smoothly.

The day was a success. Not only had we been captivated by the beauty of Homer, but we also felt well-prepared for the days ahead. As we left the harbor, I reflected on the incredible landscapes and the warm hospitality we had already experienced. It was shaping up to be an unforgettable journey.

Homer Harbor, located on the Spit, is the largest marina I've ever seen, featuring floating docks that accommodate approximately 1,500 boats of all shapes and sizes. The tides here vary by as much as 25 feet daily. This dramatic tidal range creates challenges with the connecting ramps between the land and the marina's docks. At low tide, the steep angle of the ramps makes walking either up or down difficult until the tide rises. Navigating the marina can also be exhausting; knowing the exact dock location by slip number is critical to avoid getting lost.

The party boats that we were scheduled to use over the next few days were located on docks A and C. After speaking with Cathy at Rainbow Tours, we had the slip numbers, which saved us from aimlessly searching in the vast marina. However, we hadn't discussed parking with her, and the next morning we discovered how packed the parking lots were. Unless we arrived at the marina by 6 a.m., securing a spot near the ramps was nearly impossible. This meant we often had to park farther away, adding to the difficulty of hauling bags of food, clothes, and fishing gear to the boats.

Parking on the Spit, in general, is a challenge, whether for fishing or shopping. During both morning and afternoon hours we saw crowded lots, and the situation worsened during the peak tourist season. Summer turns Homer into a bustling destination, with the Spit springing to life, as temperatures rise and the snow melts. By late March and early April, migratory birds return, and nature awakens with vibrant greenery and wildlife activity. Halibut begin migrating toward Kachemak Bay during this time, making it a prime season for anglers.

The unique estuarine environment of Kachemak Bay plays a crucial role in attracting fish such as halibut. An estuary is where freshwater from rivers mixes with ocean saltwater, creating a brackish water environment rich in nutrients. This combination supports diverse ecosystems, providing breeding grounds and nurseries for marine life. Halibut, for instance, migrate from deep oceanic waters to these nutrient-rich shallows for spawning and feeding. From April to June, they are most abundant, making this a rewarding time for fishermen.

Homer is a destination spot, especially during the summer. The Homer Spit, an extension of Homer itself, comes to life in the spring as the weather warms. Spring in Homer typically begins at the end of March, with temperatures rising, snow melting, and nature awakening. Migratory birds return to the area during this time, and by late March into April, birdwatchers can observe a variety of species, including waterfowl and seabirds.

Differences Between Waterfowl and Seabirds

Waterfowl and seabirds differ in their habitats, adaptations, and behaviors:

1. **Habitat:**

    - **Waterfowl:** Generally found in freshwater environments like lakes, rivers, marshes, and ponds. Examples include ducks, geese, and swans.

    - **Seabirds:** Typically inhabit coastlines or open seas in saltwater environments. Examples include gulls, pelicans, puffins, and albatrosses.

2. **Adaptations:**

    - **Waterfowl:** Adapted for freshwater, many have webbed feet for swimming and filter-feeding structures for sifting food from mud or water.

    - **Seabirds:** Specialized for ocean life, with salt glands to excrete excess salt and wings suited for long-distance flights over open water. Many are adept divers to catch fish.

3. **Diet and Foraging:**

    - **Waterfowl:** Mostly feed on aquatic plants, small fish, invertebrates, and insects, often foraging on or near the water's surface.

    - **Seabirds:** Primarily fish-eaters, diving to catch prey.

They may also scavenge or hunt small marine animals.

4. **Behavior and Life Cycle:**

- **Waterfowl:** Migrate seasonally between freshwater bodies, often traveling shorter distances than seabirds.
- **Seabirds:** Known for long migrations, some covering thousands of miles annually, such as the Arctic tern, which migrates between the Arctic and Antarctic.

In summary, waterfowl are freshwater birds adapted to ponds, lakes, and rivers, while seabirds thrive along coastlines and open seas.

THE RETURN OF MARINE LIFE

Spring also marks the return of marine life, including salmon, which begin moving closer to shore in late April or May. Halibut start migrating toward Kachemak Bay as early as late March to early April, moving from deeper oceanic waters (200–1,000 feet or more) into shallower areas for spawning. Kachemak Bay, an estuary where freshwater from rivers mixes with saltwater, provides a nutrient-rich environment that supports a diverse ecosystem, attracting halibut and other marine life.

Estuaries like Kachemak Bay play a crucial role in coastal ecosystems by:

- Supporting diverse plants and animals adapted to varying salinity.

- Acting as natural filters, trapping pollutants and sediments.
- Protecting inland areas from storm surges and flooding.

Halibut are particularly abundant from April to June, making them a prime target for recreational and commercial fishermen. They often inhabit sandy or muddy bottoms in the bay, hunting flatfish, crabs, and other bottom-dwelling organisms.

SPRING EVENTS AND TOURISM

Homer hosts local events and festivals celebrating the season, such as the Homer Winter Carnival in early March and the Kachemak Bay Shorebird Festival in May. The Homer Spit reaches its peak vibrancy in May, making it an ideal time for visitors to enjoy the area's natural beauty and diverse wildlife.

With the arrival of spring, everything feels new—the ice melts, temperatures rise, plants bloom, and wildlife awakens. Bears emerge from hibernation, and salmon begin their journey upriver. Visitors interested in camping or securing recreational vehicle sites must book early due to the high demand.

SEASONAL POPULATION CHANGES

As of the 2020 Census, Homer had a population of approximately 5,400 residents. This number fluctuates significantly with the influx of seasonal residents and tourists. During summer (May to September), the population nearly doubles, driven by visitors seeking outdoor activities, natural beauty, and local events. Seasonal workers also contribute to the increase. In contrast, the population drops to around 3,000–4,000 during winter, as tourists and seasonal workers leave and residents reduce outdoor activities due to harsh weather.

SUMMER ON THE HOMER SPIT

During the summer, the roads become congested with all types of vehicles, from cars and trucks to recreational vehicles and motorcycles, each more unique than the last. Sitting at a roadside restaurant along the Sterling Highway (Alaska Route 1), sipping coffee or eating ice cream, offers a front-row seat to this parade of vehicular ingenuity. Traffic can be bumper-to-bumper, requiring extra caution when crossing the road. Despite the congestion, drivers are surprisingly polite.

Parking on the Spit typically costs $10 a day, so it's wise to be prepared to walk to your destination. Fortunately, there are plenty of public restrooms, retail stores, and restaurants along the way. The Spit's activity slows by September 6 as stores close for the season, anticipating bad weather.

Activities on Homer Spit

Homer Spit is a unique and scenic destination offering activities for locals and tourists alike. Fishing is one of the most popular activities, with opportunities for saltwater fishing, including halibut, salmon, and rockfish. Many charter companies operate from the Spit, providing guided fishing trips.

Fishing

Saltwater fishing is a major draw, with numerous charter companies offering trips for halibut, salmon, and rockfish. Popular options include:

- **Rainbow Tours** (907-235-7272): Specializes in fishing and wildlife tours.
- **Homer Ocean Charters** (907-235-3232): Provides guided fishing experiences.
- **North Country Charters** (800-770-7620): Offers small-group trips for a personalized fishing experience.

Additionally, public fishing areas like the **Nick Dudiak Fishing Lagoon** and the **Spit Fishing Pier** allow anglers to fish without a boat. These spots are excellent for catching salmon during their runs.

WILDLIFE VIEWING

The Spit is a haven for birdwatchers and marine life enthusiasts. Shorebirds, seabirds, and waterfowl can be spotted, alongside sea otters, seals, and even whales. Guided wildlife tours from companies like **Ashore Water Taxi** (907-235-2341) and **Seabird Ventures** (907-435-4030) provide opportunities to observe Alaska's incredible biodiversity.

KAYAKING AND PADDLEBOARDING

Exploring Kachemak Bay by kayak or paddleboard is a popular activity. Companies like **True North Kayak Adventures** (907-299-3299) offer guided tours and rentals, allowing visitors to paddle through serene waters while observing wildlife.

SHOPPING AND DINING

The Spit's many shops and restaurants cater to tourists, offering local crafts, art, and fresh seafood. Notable spots include:

- **Salty Dawg Saloon:** A historic bar with a quirky charm, known for its dollar-bill-covered walls.
- **Captain Pattie's Fish House:** Renowned for its fresh seafood.
- **Two Sisters Bakery:** A cozy spot for pastries and coffee.

CAMPING AND OUTDOOR ACTIVITIES

Campgrounds like **Homer Spit Campground** and **Heritage RV Park** provide options for those who wish to stay close to the bay. These sites offer picnic areas, beach access, and opportunities for activities like hiking and birdwatching.

Exploring Homer Spit is an unforgettable experience, blending the rugged beauty of Alaska with a vibrant community and endless recreational opportunities. Its unique natural setting, paired with diverse activities, makes it a must-visit destination for anyone seeking adventure or relaxation.

FISHING CHARTER COMPANIES IN HOMER, ALASKA

These companies offer a range of fishing experiences, from halibut to salmon charters, and are known for their knowledgeable crews and commitment to providing memorable fishing adventures. For more details, visit their respective websites or contact them directly.

ALASKA COASTAL MARINE

- **Phone:** (907) 235-8040
- **Address:** 4287 Homer Spit Rd, Homer, AK 99603
- **Website:** https://halibutfishinghomeralaska.com/

HOMER HALIBUT HUNTERS

- **Phone:** (907) 302-4124
- **Address:** 3874 Homer Spit Rd, Homer, AK 99603
- **Website:** https://homerhalibuthunters.com/

HOMER OCEAN CHARTERS

- **Phone:** (907) 235-3232
- **Address:** 4305 Homer Spit Rd, Homer, AK 99603
- **Website:** https://www.homerocean.com/

MAVERICK CHARTERS

- **Phone:** (907) 235-8792
- **Address:** 4246 Homer Spit Rd #1, Homer, AK 99603
- **Website:** https://www.maverickcharters.com/

NORTH COUNTRY CHARTERS

- **Phone:** (800) 770-7620
- **Address:** 4287 Homer Spit Rd, Homer, AK 99603
- **Website:** https://www.northcountrycharters.com/

O'FISH'IAL CHARTERS

- **Phone:** (907) 435-4444
- **Address:** 2301 Kachemak Dr, Homer, AK 99603
- **Website:** https://bighalibut.com/

RAINBOW TOURS

- **Phone:** (907) 235-7272
- **Address:** 4287 Homer Spit Rd, Homer, AK 99603
- **Website:** https://www.rainbowtours.net/

PIER FISHING LOCATIONS

Public fishing areas on the Spit, including the famous Homer Spit Fishing Pier, allow individuals to fish without requiring a boat. Here are notable spots:

NICK DUDIAK FISHING LAGOON

- **Description:** Known as "The Fishing Hole," this lagoon is a popular destination for anglers. It is stocked with salmon fry, providing access to king salmon (May–early July) and silver salmon (mid-July–September).
- **Facilities:** Handicap-accessible platform, parking, fish cleaning tables, restrooms, picnic areas.
- **Best for:** Family-friendly shore fishing.

HOMER SPIT FISHING PIER

- **Description:** Offers opportunities to catch halibut, rockfish, and salmon. Located close to the ocean, it provides both deep-sea and shore fishing experiences.
- **Facilities:** Parking, easy water access.

HOMER SPIT BEACHES

- **Description:** An informal but excellent option for shore fishing, particularly during salmon runs. Peak fishing yields exciting results.

WILDLIFE VIEWING LOCATIONS

ALASKA ISLANDS & OCEAN VISITOR CENTER

- **Description:** Features exhibits on local wildlife, including seabirds, marine mammals, and terrestrial species. Offers guided tours.
- **Best Season:** Year-round, especially spring and summer for bird migrations.
- **Phone:** (907) 235-6961
- **Address:** 95 Sterling Hwy, Suite 1, Homer, AK 99603

KACHEMAK BAY STATE PARK

- **Description:** Known for diverse wildlife, including sea otters and seals. Offers outdoor recreational opportunities.
- **Best Season:** Spring and summer (May–August).
- **Phone:** (907) 235-7024
- **Address:** 95 Sterling Hwy, Suite 2, Homer, AK 99603

HOMER SPIT

- **Description:** Spot birds, marine life, and tide pools.
- **Best Season:** Spring and summer during migratory periods.
- **Phone:** (907) 226-3180
- **Address:** 3232 Homer Spit Rd, Homer, AK 99603

NICK DUDIAK FISHING LAGOON (THE FISHING HOLE)

- **Description:** During salmon runs (May–September), it's an excellent spot for observing fish and associated wildlife like birds and bears.
- **Phone:** (907) 235-3170
- **Address:** Near Homer Small Boat Harbor, Homer, AK 99603

SHOPPING IN HOMER AND HOMER SPIT

CLASSIC COOK

- **Phone:** (907) 435-0668
- **Address:** 378 East Pioneer Avenue, Homer, AK 99603
- **Description:** Offers kitchenware, gadgets, and culinary classes.

INUA

- **Phone:** (907) 235-7075
- **Address:** 4287 Homer Spit Rd, Homer, AK 99603
- **Description:** Features Alaska crafts and artwork, including jewelry and carvings.

NORTH WIND HOME COLLECTION

- **Phone:** (907) 235-0766
- **Address:** 173 West Pioneer Avenue, Homer, AK 99603
- **Description:** Offers home décor, furniture, and textiles.

SALMON SISTERS

- **Phone:** (907) 235-5555
- **Address:** 1554 Spit Road, Homer, AK 99603
- **Description:** Specializes in Alaskan-themed products, apparel, and gifts.

THE ART SHOP GALLERY

- **Phone:** (907) 235-7076
- **Address:** 202 W Pioneer Ave, Suite A, Homer, AK 99603
- **Description:** Displays local art and photography.

Camping and Outdoor Activities

Homer Spit Campground

- **Phone:** (907) 235-1583
- **Address:** 4611 Homer Spit Rd, Homer, AK 99603
- **Description:** Beachfront campsites with picnic areas, ideal for fishing and kayaking.

Heritage RV Park

- **Phone:** (907) 226-4500
- **Address:** 3350 Homer Spit Rd, Homer, AK 99603
- **Description:** Offers full hookups and stunning bay views.

Homer / Baycrest KOA

- **Phone:** (907) 235-8675
- **Address:** 4545 Kenai Spur Hwy, Homer, AK 99603
- **Description:** Provides tent sites, RV sites, and cabins.

Kayak Adventures

Here are some companies offering kayaking adventures in Homer, Alaska:

TRUE NORTH KAYAK ADVENTURES

- **Phone:** (907) 299-3299
- **Address:** 1512 E. End Rd, Homer, AK 99603
- **Website:** https://truenorthkayak.com/
- **Details:** Offers half-day, full-day, and multi-day guided trips in Kachemak Bay, emphasizing safe paddling practices and equipment rentals.

ST. AUGUSTINE'S KAYAK & TOURS

- **Phone:** (907) 235-5680
- **Address:** 4306 Homer Spit Rd, Homer, AK 99603
- **Website:** www.kachemakbayadventures.com/
- **Details:** Provides half-day and full-day kayaking tours, focusing on wildlife viewing and the area's unique ecosystems.

THREE MOOSE KAYAK ADVENTURES

- **Phone:** (907) 299-0150
- **Address:** 2941 N. Fork Rd, Homer, AK 99603
- **Website:** https://threemoose.com/
- **Details:** Specializes in guided kayaking and hiking tours, exploring the stunning scenery of Kachemak Bay for all skill levels.

KACHEMAK BAY ADVENTURES

- **Phone:** (907) 235-9119
- **Address:** 2201 Kachemak Dr, Homer, AK 99603
- **Website:** https://www.kachemakbayadventures.com/
- **Details:** Offers custom kayaking tours, rentals, and water taxi services to remote locations.

INLET CHARTERS ACROSS ALASKA ADVENTURES

- **Phone:** (907) 435-1600
- **Address:** 4287 Homer Spit Rd #7, Homer, AK 99603
- **Website:** https://halibutcharters.com/
- **Details:** Provides guided sea kayaking trips and fishing charters, focusing on wildlife and natural beauty.

OTHER NOTABLE EXPERIENCES

KACHEMAK BAY ADVENTURES

- **Phone:** (907) 235-9119
- **Address:** 2201 Kachemak Dr, Homer, AK 99603
- **Website:** https://www.kachemakbayadventures.com/
- **Details:** Specializes in birdwatching and hiking tours, including scenic trips to Grewingk Glacier Lake.

ALASKA BEAR ADVENTURES

- **Phone:** Toll-Free: 1-877-522-9247 | Local: (907) 299-5229
- **Office Address:** 4287 Homer Spit Rd #9, Homer, AK 99603
- **Hanger Address:** 2282 Kachemak Dr, Homer, AK 99603
- **Website:**
- **Details:** Offers bear-viewing excursions with a focus on safety and education.

HOMER SPIT CAMPGROUND

- **Phone:** (907) 235-8206
- **Address:** 4535 Homer Spit Rd, Homer, AK 99603
- **Website:** www.homerspitcampground.com/
- **Details:** A great base for fishing, hiking, and wildlife watching.

ALASKA WILDLIFE CONSERVATION CENTER

- **Phone:** (907) 783-0058
- **Address:** 43520 Seward Hwy, Girdwood, AK 99587
- **Website:** https://alaskawildlife.org/
- **Details:** Offers a chance to see native wildlife, including moose, bears, and bison.

BREWERY TOURS

HOMER BREWING COMPANY

- **Phone:** (907) 235-3626
- **Address:** 1411 Lakeshore Dr, Homer, AK 99603
- **Website:** www.homerbrew.com/
- **Details:** Showcases the craft beer scene in Homer through tours and tastings.

CULTURAL EXPERIENCES

THE PRATT MUSEUM

Σ **Phone:** (907) 235-8635
- **Address:** 3779 Bartlett St, Homer, AK 99603
- **Website:** www.prattmuseum.org/
- **Details:** Explores the culture, science, and art of the Kachemak Bay area through exhibits and outdoor displays.

ALASKA ISLANDS & OCEAN VISITOR CENTER

- **Phone:** (907) 235-6961
- **Address:** 95 Sterling Hwy, Suite 1, Homer, AK 99603
- **Website:** www.fws.gov/refuge/alaska-maritime/visit-us
- **Details:** Offers interpretive exhibits and guided tours to explore the Alaska Maritime National Wildlife Refuge.

NOTABLE LANDMARK

SALTY DAWG SALOON

- **Phone:** (907) 235-6718
- **Address:** 4380 Homer Spit Rd, Homer, AK 99603
- **Details:** A historic bar known for its rustic charm. The Salty Dawg Saloon dates back to 1897 when it was initially built as one of the first cabins in Homer. The cabin served multiple purposes over the years, including being the first post office, a grocery store, and even an office for coal mining.

In the late 1940s, Chuck Abbott acquired the cabin. In 1949, he and his friend Gerald Gifford moved the cabin to its current location on the Homer Spit. The establishment officially opened as the Salty Dawg Saloon in 1957. By 1960, the saloon had expanded with an adjacent building, coinciding with Alaska's statehood. The saloon is known for its rustic charm, quirky decor, and the tradition of patrons tacking

signed dollar bills to the walls. This tradition began when a visitor left a dollar bill for a friend, and it has since become a popular practice among visitors. The bar has also gained recognition through its appearances on television shows like *Deadliest Catch*.

The Salty Dawg Saloon has a rich history that reflects the development of Homer, Alaska. Before the 1964 Good Friday Earthquake, the saloon was originally located at the end of the Homer Spit, housed in a cabin built in 1897. This cabin served multiple purposes over the years, including being a post office and a general store. The building has historical significance, as it is believed to be one of the earliest structures in the area, with ties to the coal mining activities of the early 20th century.

After the 1964 earthquake, which caused significant structural damage, the saloon was moved to its present location near the small boat harbor. Its current address is 4380 Homer Spit Rd, Homer. This location offers easy access for visitors and stunning views of Kachemak Bay. The relocation of the Salty Dawg Saloon not only preserved its legacy but also allowed it to continue serving the community and visitors. Today, it is a beloved landmark known for its unique atmosphere and history, attracting many who want to experience a piece of Alaskan culture.

The saloon provides a lively atmosphere with a variety of drinks, including local beers and cocktails. It's a great place for both locals and tourists to gather, enjoy live music, and savor the unique character of this historic saloon while taking in views of the surrounding waters and wildlife.

When we were done speaking with Kathy from Rainbow Tours, about our fishing itinerary that we signed up for, the location of the boats in the harbor and parking arrangements for the day, we decided to wander around the Spit to browse the many stores. There were stores on both sides of the Sterling Highway.

As we drove south about two miles, we ended at the very tip of the Spit, which is marked by a huge hotel called **Land's End**. This three-story building at the tip of the Spit overlooks the Kachemak Bay and the magnificent Kenai Mountains behind the bay—a fabulous view that would have cost $350 a night if we wished to stay there. The hotel was built on the banks of the bay with endless views of the waters and mountains. Just breathtaking. It was a sight to behold, and one could see all the boats leaving the Homer Harbor. Small boats and large boats were coming in and out of the harbor. And, as is customary for the crew, filleting the fish caught and discarding the carcass into the water while making the trip back to shore on the aft deck of the boat brought a fascinating spectacle. Hundreds of white seagulls followed the boat, diving into the water to collect the debris—a phenomenally impressive and eye-catching sight. We were lucky to witness it.

There were also fish under the boat helping themselves to the scraps of fish being thrown overboard, and one could see the churning water as they jumped out. As the party boats were coming into Homer Harbor and making their way into the marina to dock, it was a chaotic scene, almost like the Alfred Hitchcock movie *The Birds*, with diving birds from the sky into the water and fish under the boat jumping up and churning it. Imagine a thousand birds diving and sitting on the water, waiting for scraps of food.

As the fishing boats came closer to the entrance of the harbor, where the distance between the boat and land narrowed, many fishermen with long poles were trying to cast into the chaotic pool of fish, where the birds were diving. The fishermen were using the birds as decoys to catch the pollock swimming in the water. What a sight to see—just unimaginable. There were birds, fish, fishing boats, and fishermen all within a very short distance of each other. The fishermen were aggressive, wearing long boots and waders, walking as deep as they could into the water so that when they cast their rods, the line would land near all the commotion out there. The deeper they could move into the water, the easier it would be for their lines to reach the fish.

Some of these fishermen had extremely long fishing poles, 15 to 18 feet tall, with large spinning reels—absolutely amazing. They were catching fish doing this, mostly pollock with a few other species. A pollock is a beautiful fish, part of the scrod family. As I watched this, I also walked to the banks to see and study their catch. I realized there were a lot of fish to catch in these waters.

It was getting late now, even though the day was as bright as could be, because the sun wouldn't set until around 11 p.m. We were feeling a bit tired, having traveled from Anchorage that morning and having done a lot in between. So, we decided to start heading back to the town of Homer and off the Spit. We walked up the rocky slopes of the bank of the Kachemak Bay, occasionally bending down to pick up black and gray rocks as souvenirs to take home.

We entered our cute little Ford SUV and started driving north, back to Homer through the Spit. It would take us about 25 minutes to get back home. The journey, once we reached the mainland off the Spit, was only about five miles. I was anxious to have dinner and get to bed as early as possible because tomorrow we would  be returning to the Spit to go on our first fishing trip in the Bay of Alaska. As we were heading out, I thought of how wonderful it would be to fish off the banks, like the other fishermen, and catch pollock. I planned to come back to this same spot and bring my own spinning rod. I couldn't wait to try it myself.

CHAPTER 14

JULY 25

I laid in bed skimming through articles in *The New York Times*, *The Wall Street Journal*, and our local New Jersey newspaper (*The Star-Ledger*) as well as viewing CNN World News. This is my daily morning ritual to quench my curiosity. It's a habit I've followed for years, and it makes me feel alive, keeping me informed about the issues here in the USA and around the world. This practice helps put my concerns into perspective. So often, we worry endlessly about the most trivial things, failing to recognize the bigger problems and challenges others face. It's similar to the idea of someone preoccupied with their own problems until they meet someone whose struggles are far greater. That kind of realization, knowing what's happening in other countries or even within our own, and how it affects others, helps minimize our own little worries.

After about an hour, I put down my phone and got out of bed, ready to face the day's challenges—and have some fun. I was particularly excited because today marked the first day of our fishing excursion in Homer's Kachemak Bay. After getting dressed and enjoying a cup of coffee, I sat at the dining room table in our charming Airbnb. While sipping my coffee, I checked my emails and texts. Once I cleared most of the items off my to-do list, I felt ready to start the day. It was already 8 a.m., and I realized how quickly the morning had passed.

As we pulled out of the driveway, we could see South Peninsula Hospital, perched two blocks away atop a hill. I remembered hearing helicopters overhead the previous day, likely landing on the hospital rooftop to save someone's life. Talking to the locals, I learned that the hospital is highly respected in Homer and has an excellent reputation. It handles all sorts of serious cases, and for anything beyond its capabilities, patients are flown to Anchorage via helicopter for urgent or emergent care. While South Peninsula Hospital might seem small compared to Community Medical Center in Toms River, New Jersey, it is a significant facility for this area. Its location on a hill makes it one of the taller buildings in Homer, and from its vantage point, you can enjoy the best view in town. From there, the Homer Spit stretches out magnificently—it almost makes you regret not being sick enough to be admitted just to enjoy the incredible view.

As we turned out of the driveway, the Kenai Mountains loomed ahead of us. We drove down the hill and onto US-1 South, also known as the Sterling Highway. Heading toward the Homer Spit, the drive was nothing short of breathtaking, with Kachemak Bay on both sides of the highway and the Kenai Mountains straight ahead, giving the impression that the road would plunge directly into the bay at its end. With about three hours to kill before boarding our fishing boat, *Foxfire*, we decided to spend some time exploring and investigating the Spit.

Beluga Lake

The scenery was stunning, with water on all sides, majestic mountains, and vibrant plant life. Driving down the highway's southern side, we passed a place called Lake Beluga, primarily used by floatplanes, or bush planes, which carry people on excursions around Homer. The roadside vegetation was lush and vibrant, with hues of green, pink, purple, and white from various flowers and grasses blanketing the ground. The standout plants that morning were the towering cow parsnips.

These cow parsnips were interspersed with radiant yellow **hawksbeards**, vivid pink **fireweed**, and blue-purple **lupines**. White-headed **yarrow** plants and the occasional goldenrods added further diversity to the kaleidoscope of colors. The vegetation was so abundant it felt as if we were driving through a carefully curated garden, with the mountains and bay providing a perfect backdrop.

Cow parsnip, native to Alaska, is both a blessing and a potential nuisance, depending on where it grows. While it provides habitat and food for wildlife, its rapid growth and large size can crowd out other plants, leading some to label it a weed. The plant contains furanocoumarins, which can cause skin irritation when its sap is exposed to sunlight, so I made a mental note to avoid handling it directly. In its natural environment, however, cow parsnip plays an essential role, particularly in Alaska's coastal areas and forests. Its widespread growth in Homer is so characteristic that it's hard to imagine the area without it.

Despite its classification as a weed by some, I found cow parsnip to be absolutely beautiful. The plant stands tall and grows in impressive clusters, giving Homer a unique charm. I love looking at them. If ever there were a plant to change someone's mind about weeds being ugly, cow parsnip would be it.

I was already so excited as we drove down the Sterling Highway, surrounded by vibrant plants. The thought of fishing at the end of the Spit, off the banks with my spinning reels, filled me with anticipation. I envisioned myself just like the other fishermen I had seen the previous day, catching pollock while wading into the water with their boots and waders. It had been so fascinating to watch them aim for the areas where birds were diving to catch their own food.

Today it would be my turn. The early morning traffic was light, and it didn't take long to reach the end of the road at the Spit. The drive itself was serene, and as soon as we arrived, I could hardly contain my excitement. It was already 9 a.m. when we parked the car near the bank. I quickly assembled my three-piece fishing pole, which had traveled with us all the way from New Jersey. We brought two poles and they had already proven their worth on the Alagnak River, where Laurie and I had caught at least 100 pounds of sockeye salmon.

Carefully, I pieced the rods together and tied a medium-sized, silver-green, shiny metal lure to the PowerPro fishing line. With great caution, I walked down the bank, mindful of the small, round volcanic and marine stones underfoot. These smooth gray and black stones, likely centuries old, were slippery and uneven, so I moved deliberately to avoid twisting my ankle and jeopardizing the rest of my trip.

Since I didn't have boots or waders, I stayed at the edge of the water, ensuring my clothing stayed dry. I chose a spot on the bank, far enough from other fishermen, to avoid accidentally hooking anyone. With all my strength and focus, I cast my line as far as I could. The lure landed near the wading and diving birds in the water. I silently congratulated myself for doing a good job casting my line successfully.

Within moments, I felt a nibble, then a solid bite. I lifted the rod's tip towards the sky and with a quick jerk, and started reeling the line in as fast as I could. In my excitement, I barely noticed how quickly I reeled in the line until it suddenly bounced onto the rocky shore. As the fish thrashed on the bank, I saw that I had hooked it right in the mouth. It was a beautiful fish, shimmering with colors I hadn't seen before. I called out to a nearby fisherman to identify it, and he responded, "Nice pollock!"

This was my first pollock, and I was captivated. The pollock, part of the scrod family, is a significant fish in both commercial fishing and culinary circles. Typically, pollock have a torpedo-shaped body with dark gray to silvery scales, and they can grow from one to four feet long, reaching weights of up to 40 pounds. They are semi-pelagic, often found in the mid-layers of the ocean, swimming in large schools. Their diet consists of smaller fish, zooplankton, and krill during their early life stages, shifting to larger prey as they grow.

Pollock are vital to Alaska's commercial fishing industry. The Alaska pollock fishery is known for its sustainable practices, with populations carefully monitored to prevent overfishing. Pollock are widely used in fish fillets, surimi (processed seafood), and fast-food items like fish sandwiches. Their mild flavor and flaky texture make them versatile in many dishes, including sushi and fish and chips.

As I marveled at my catch, I couldn't help but recall that **pollock** is related to **cod** and **haddock**, which are part of the **scrod family**. These fish share a reputation for their mild flavor and tender, flaky flesh. Atlantic cod, found in the North Atlantic, is renowned for its use in dishes like fish and chips and chowder. Haddock, slightly sweeter than cod, is distinctive for the black line running along its side. It is often baked or fried.

Standing there with my first Homer pollock, I felt a deep sense of accomplishment. The beauty of the fish and the excitement of the moment would stay with me forever, just like any "first" that holds a special place in one's memory.

HADDOCK

PACIFIC COD

POLLOCK

I remember going out to dinner a while ago and seeing pollock on the menu. I had no idea what kind of fish it was. I discovered that pollock is part of the scrod family. When in restaurants, I realized that "scrod" is not a precise scientific designation but rather a more generic and loose term used in restaurant lingo, meaning "catch of the day," not applying the name to pollock, haddock or cod. So do not confuse that term with its real meaning.

When asked, many servers are unsure and unable to provide a clear answer to the question, often not fully understanding the distinction themselves. Therefore, an encounter with "scrod" on a menu typically does not indicate a specific fish from that family.

As soon as I landed the pollock, I realized that I did not have a bag to put him in. In an excited state, I ran to the car trying to find one. Again, I kept reminding myself to be careful not to hurt myself on these round stones.

I found a bag in the car and then ran down the embankment again to place this gorgeous fish into it. As I ran back up the bank with the pollock in the bag I was holding, I could not help but notice the beautiful small and medium-sized stones that lay in my path. So even though I was somewhat worried about being late to our party boat, I started collecting some of the stones and placing them in my pockets. I wanted to take them home as souvenirs. I have been collecting stones from different trips for years. There were gray stones with speckles of black and white in them. They were of different sizes and shapes—unlike any I had seen before. Some stones were rusty and red, probably laden with iron or copper.

A large, shiny, polished black one caught my eyes, as black as one can imagine. Maybe this one came from the dried-up coal that was previously on the Spit, being hauled out on the departing ships. I remembered that Homer used to be a coal town, and I thought this could have been a relic from the past during that time. I picked it up and stuffed it into my pocket, along with other smaller rocks. I couldn't wait to place these rocks and stones on the mantel of my fireplace in my great room. I did the same thing when I was in

Iceland and brought some relics of ancient stones home. I collected lava stones from Iceland and old bricks dating back to the Civil War of the 1860s that I collected at Fort Jefferson at the Dry Tortugas, in the Gulf of America. They were relics of the old fort, which was built there using 16 million bricks. The fort was approximately 80 miles from Key West, where they were picked up to be delivered for its construction. I find that these relics have a way of speaking to me, talking when I get them home.

Time was running short, and we had to head north on the Sterling Highway to board the party boat. The *Spirit* was scheduled to leave promptly at 12 p.m., and we knew it wouldn't wait for any latecomers. I therefore in anticipation made my way back to the car. I loaded my spinning reels and rods into the trunk. I placed the bag with the pollock inside an area where it would not drip inside it because I did not want the vehicle to smell of fish. It was a rental car, and I needed to be extra careful to return it in the same manner that it had been received. We left this area known as the Land's End Hotel and headed north to the *Spirit*. We now knew where to park.

We still had to find the ramp and the dock leading to the boat. The angle of the ramp was very steep now because the tide was low. If I could have measured the angle with

a level, I suspect it would have been around 35 degrees. I had to be careful going down, to avoid sliding or tripping. I braced myself using the side rale going down to steady my gate.

As we walked down this steep ramp, we were looking for the *Spirit*. The *Spirit* a monohull boat was 65 feet long and 20 feet wide and had the legal capacity to carry 25 passengers. It was Rainbow's contractor for the afternoon fishing trips. It would leave at 12 p.m. sharp and return to shore after piloting us thru the Kachemak Bay for about 25 miles and when out of this bay it would head north to the Gulf of Alaska. Past the Gulf, laid the North Pacific Ocean. Some days the boat with its crew and passengers would return earlier than 6 p.m., this would have happened if all the passengers caught their maximum fish bag limit for the day. Each passenger was allowed to keep two halibuts per day. One had to be under 28 inches and the second any other size smaller or larger than 28 inches. The reason for this was to give the bigger halibuts a chance to reproduce and repopulate the species. The population of halibuts as a whole is very tightly watched and regulated by the government, and being a federally regulated fish, there is no halibut fishing on Wednesdays. On Wednesdays, any boat leaving the dock is going to fish for any other species than halibut. That leaves the fishing to salmon, cod, haddock, pollock and rockfish. This way, future generations of halibuts can survive and be sustained. I was happy to learn the conservation methods and techniques in Homer for halibuts.

Captain James and first mate Patrick on the Spirit. They took us fishing for a half day on the Spirit boat. The handheld Garmin radio showing the Alaska Maine Highway in Kachemak Bay. Those folks are either feeling tired or sick. What do you think?

Once on the dock, we located the *Spirit* and used its ramp to get on. We were on time and were ready to be taken out to fish.

The Kachemak Bay surrounds the northwestern part of the Kenai Mountains, whose snowy white peaks and massive glaciers are visible from miles away. These mountains, gleaming like a necklace encircling the bay, create a mesmerizing backdrop. For millennia, the bay has drawn people to its shores, providing resources and sustenance. Its richness stems from its diverse topography, abundant plant and animal life, unique geology, and varying climates along its northern and southern shores. Human life in the area has always been deeply tied to the Kachemak Bay, with the earliest settlements located along the water's edge.

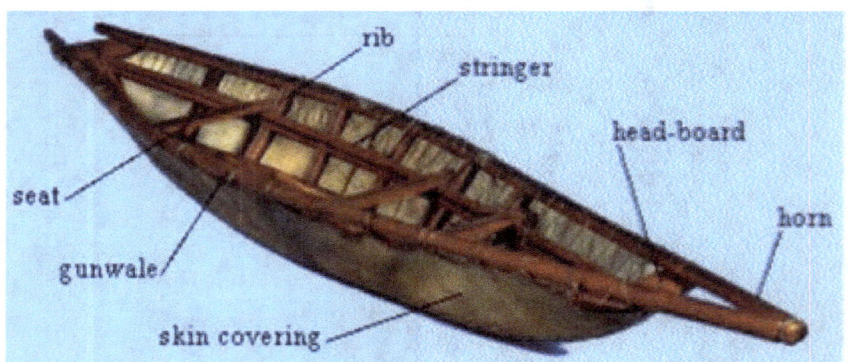

The first residents arrived in kayaks and larger umiaks, settling near the water and relying on it for travel and sustenance. They harvested edible plants and animals from intertidal zones hunted seals, sea otters, porpoises, and beluga whales in nearshore waters;

and fished in deeper parts of the bay. They also gathered seabird eggs, chicks, and adults from rookeries on steep-sided islands.

WHAT IS A ROOKERY?

A rookery is a breeding colony or nesting area where large numbers of animals, particularly birds or marine mammals, gather to mate, give birth, and care for their young. Originally used to describe nesting areas of rooks (a type of crow), the term now encompasses various species.

COMMON TYPES OF ROOKERIES INCLUDE:

- **Bird Rookeries:** Seabirds like puffins, herons, or pelicans often nest in colonies on cliffs, islands, or wetlands, which provide protection from predators.

- **Marine Mammal Rookeries:** Coastal areas or ice flows where seals, sea lions, or walruses give birth and raise their young.

- Rookeries are vital for species survival, offering safety and creating social structures necessary for breeding and rearing offspring.

LIFE ONSHORE

Onshore, the early inhabitants of Kachemak Bay collected plants, caught salmon in freshwater streams, and found temporary shelter in rock niches. They hunted caribou, Dall sheep, bears, marmots, foxes, and birds for sustenance. They also utilized natural materials to create tools and ornaments:

- **Chert** was used for arrowheads, knives, and spear points.

  Characteristics of Chert:
  - A hard, fine-grained sedimentary rock primarily composed of quartz.
  - Forms in marine environments, often from silica-rich organisms like diatoms.
  - Known for its hardness and ability to produce sharp edges, making it ideal for ancient tools.
  - Found in various colors, including gray, brown, black, and red.

- **Shale** was baked to create beads and tiny figurines.

  Characteristics of Shale:

  - A fine-grained sedimentary rock formed from compacted mud and clay.
  - Laminated structure, splitting into thin, parallel layers.
  - Found in colors like gray, black, brown, red, and green, depending on its mineral content.
  - Used historically and industrially in cement and ceramics and as a source of natural gas and oil.

- Rounded beach boulders and pebbles were fashioned into fishing weights.

THE ARRIVAL OF THE RUSSIANS

In the late 1700s, Russian explorers arrived in the area, drawn by the aquatic wealth of the bay. They primarily sought the pelts of sea otters, a highly valuable commodity. They also observed schools of herring in Seldovia Bay and discovered coal deposits near the Homer Spit.

AMERICAN SETTLEMENT

Following the purchase of Alaska by the United States in 1867, Americans slowly ventured northward. They crossed the North Pacific by boat, bringing new industries and settlements to

Kachemak Bay. Over time, the region's rich natural resources and captivating landscapes continued to attract people, cementing its place as a hub of history, culture, and natural wonder.

The first economies of the American period in the Kachemak Bay area were rooted in coal and gold mining, fishing, agriculture, and fur farming. During the first eight decades of the 20th century, the development of various fisheries became a primary focus for residents. These fisheries capitalized on the bay's abundant resources, including herring, halibut, salmon, shrimp, crabs, and clams.

Seldovia served as the social, religious, and economic center of Kachemak Bay until the mid-1960s. This waterfront community was oriented around water-based activities, with homes and businesses lining the shoreline. Residents traveled primarily on foot or by boat, dining on foods harvested from the nearby beaches, forests, and waters.

Long before its official naming in 1896, Homer was known as a coal community. Over time, it transformed into a fishing and farming hub. The construction of the Sterling Highway around 1950 and the opening of the small boat harbor in 1964 marked a turning point, solidifying Homer's role as the economic, cultural, and recreational center of Kachemak Bay, replacing Seldovia in prominence.

The *Spirit* had a captain and two crew members who managed most of the work involved in helping passengers fish. Homer, known as the "Halibut Capital of the World," attracts countless visitors eager to fish for this prized species. This kept the crew busy, ensuring a smooth and successful experience for everyone on board.

The interior of the boat featured two tables accommodating six people, with three seats on each side, and additional bench seating without tables. However, one notable safety concern was a step leading into the cabin from the stern. This step created a significant drop that posed a trip hazard. The issue could easily have been addressed by installing a small ramp to create a gentle slope or placing a large, visible "Watch Your Step" sign.

Unfortunately, despite the captain's warnings during the safety briefing, the step caused accidents. I witnessed an older man take a hard fall upon entering the cabin, landing on his face. He quickly stood up, perhaps out of shock and embarrassment, but it was a sobering moment. Each time I boarded the *Spirit*, I had to remind myself to be cautious when stepping inside. Though I meant to share my suggestion with the crew, the excitement of fishing distracted me, and I forgot to bring it up.

HALIBUT: A DEEP DIVE INTO THEIR BIOLOGY

As Homer is renowned for halibut fishing, I was eager to learn more about this fascinating fish.

PHYSICAL CHARACTERISTICS:

- The Pacific halibut is the largest member of the flatfish family, with a diamond-shaped body and crescent-shaped tail that distinguish it from other flatfish. They are cold-water bottom dwellers, typically found on the seafloor at depths of 20–1,000 feet, most abundantly at 100–600 feet.

LIFE CYCLE AND REPRODUCTION:

- Halibut spawn in deep waters (600–1,500 feet) from December to February, near the continental shelf's edge. Males reach sexual maturity at 7–8 years, while females take longer, maturing at 8–12 years. Mature females can lay up to four million eggs annually, with older, larger fish producing more eggs. Halibut larvae float in ocean currents for about six months, during which their left eye migrates to the right side of their head, a hallmark of flatfish.

HABITAT AND MIGRATION:

- Juvenile halibut spend 5–7 years in shallow nursery grounds before migrating clockwise in the northern Pacific. Adults prefer deeper waters and migrate less, except during mating season when they seek deeper areas for spawning.

FEEDING AND BEHAVIOR:

- Halibut are opportunistic feeders, preying on bottom-dwelling species like cod, pollock, octopus, shrimp, and crab. They are also known to swim into open water to hunt pelagic fish like salmon and herring. Their dark topside camouflages with the ocean floor, while their white underside blends with the sky when seen from below, aiding in both hunting and avoiding predators.

THREATS AND CONSERVATION:

- Halibut face threats from overfishing, habitat disruption from trawl nets, and global warming, which has been linked to a decrease in their average size. Strict regulations, including catch limits and sustainable fishing methods, have helped maintain healthy populations.

HALIBUT FISHING TECHNIQUES

The fishing method used on the *Spirit* reflects standard practices in Alaska. A typical rig includes a circle hook tied to a thick monofilament line, with a sinker weight adjusted based on current and tide conditions. Because halibut dwell on the ocean floor, the bait must reach the bottom or hover slightly above it.

When the current is strong, heavier sinkers are used to keep the bait in position. On calmer days, lighter weights (2–3 pounds) suffice, allowing anglers to feel the fish's bite more easily.

AN EXCEPTIONAL HALIBUT ADVENTURE

Fishing in Homer is an extraordinary experience, with ample opportunities to catch halibut. The crew on the *Spirit* efficiently assists passengers, from setting up rigs to cleaning and filleting the catch. Each passenger is given two zip ties to tag their fish for identification.

Halibuts

Once the boat returns to the harbor, local fish processing companies transport the catch for vacuum packing and freezing, ensuring the fish remain fresh until they are ready to be shipped or picked up.

REFLECTIONS

The beauty of Kachemak Bay, with its majestic Kenai Mountains and distant views of Kodiak Island, adds to the unforgettable experience of fishing in Homer. The *Spirit* provides a glimpse into the rich marine ecosystem and the thrill of catching one of the Pacific's most iconic fish.

The fishing setup we used was designed for efficiency and strength, perfect for catching halibut in Alaskan waters. The thicker line, shown in green within the pictures, is tied to the upper part of the lower swivel. This string is threaded through the eye of the sinker (Figure 3) and then secured back to the upper part of the swivel (Figure 4). The bottom part of the lower swivel connects to a monofilament line, which ends with a circle hook (Figure 5). This system minimizes tangles and provides the strength needed to reel in sizable halibut. The only variable is the sinker's weight, which depends on the current and wind conditions during fishing.

This is how a Halibut rig is set up. Hook, Line, and Sinker.

This system is particularly effective because it almost never allows the hook or sinker to tangle, ensuring smooth operation even under challenging conditions. Halibut bait is typically herring, though the crew often substitutes cod caught during the trip to save on the cost of herring. Herring remains the bait of choice due to its universal appeal—people and fish alike seem to love it.

A GLOBAL LOVE FOR HERRING

Reflecting on my travels, I remembered Amsterdam, where herring is a beloved staple. The city is filled with small herring carts selling sandwiches topped with pickles, a local delicacy akin to New York City's hot dog stands. Herring is as ubiquitous there, as it is in Alaska, where it serves as both bait and a culinary favorite.

THE ROLE OF TIDAL CURRENTS

Fishing during ebb tide, the period between high and low tides when the current is minimal, allowed us to drift rather than anchor. This made it easier to use lighter weights to reach the ocean floor. Tidal currents in this region are influenced by the gravitational pull of the moon and sun, creating powerful water movement as tides rise and fall.

Kachemak Bay, with its narrow shape, experiences tidal changes of up to 25 feet—a staggering difference. Water rushes rapidly between the bay and the Gulf of Alaska, creating strong currents. These conditions require fishing vessels to adapt their safety practices. Unlike in New Jersey, life buoys here are untethered, allowing for multiple quick throws in different directions during a rescue. Tethered rings would be too cumbersome in the swift currents.

Halibut: The Bottom-Dwellers

Halibut dwells near the ocean floor, typically at depths of around 200 feet. Larger halibut are often found in deeper waters, requiring more line and heavier weights to reach them. Reeling in a two-pound sinker from this depth is manageable, but the effort increases significantly with a 20-pound fish on the line.

The Difference Between Full-Day and Half-Day Trips

Booking a full-day trip with Rainbow Tours provides a unique experience compared to half-day trips. Full-day trips, on smaller 30-foot boats, accommodate only six passengers, travel farther, and fish in deeper waters, yielding larger halibut. In contrast, the larger 60-foot boats, used for half-day trips, hold up to 25 passengers and stay closer to shore. This often results in smaller fish and more frequent line tangles.

The choice between the two options often depends on the passenger's level of interest in fishing, time availability, and budget. While smaller boats offer more personal attention and fewer line tangles, larger boats provide a sense of safety and camaraderie with more passengers.

SAFETY AND LOGISTICS

Safety is a priority on all vessels, regardless of size. Both types of boats carry life vests, rings, and communication devices to ensure passenger safety. However, survival in these icy waters depends on quick action, as the cold and strong currents can be unforgiving.

Despite planning my trip months in advance, I could only secure one full-day trip due to high demand, forcing me to book several half-day trips. However, fishing in Homer proved to be an angler's paradise. Within hours, my arms grew tired from pulling up fish after fish. For those unaccustomed to daily fishing, the strain on rarely used muscles is a reminder to pace oneself.

REACHING OUR LIMIT

By early afternoon, all 25 passengers had reached their two-halibut limit, with many throwing back additional catches. The crew efficiently filleted the fish during the two-hour return trip through Kachemak Bay, ensuring the fish were cleaned, bagged, and ready upon arrival.

THE MARINE HIGHWAY AND HOMER HARBOR

Kachemak Bay is part of the Alaska Marine Highway System, a crucial waterway for transporting goods and people. The return journey offered breathtaking views of the Kenai Mountains, their peaks piercing low-lying clouds, and even distant glimpses of Kodiak Island.

Upon docking, staff from Homer Fish Processing Company greeted us, ready to transport our catch to their facility for vacuum-packing and freezing. The service was seamless and professional, providing the option to ship the fish home.

BACK ON LAND

The tide had shifted, making the ramp less steep as we disembarked. After shedding our waterproof layers, we stopped at Coal Town Coffee and Tea for a warm drink before heading back to our Airbnb on Homer's mainland.

REFLECTIONS ON AN INCREDIBLE DAY

The day had been unforgettable. From the thrill of reeling in halibut to the stunning Alaskan landscapes, it was an adventure that left me eagerly anticipating the next day. As I drifted to sleep, the soft glow of the late Alaskan evening light filled the room, a perfect end to a perfect day.

Chapter 15

July 26

A Full Day Ahead

Today was the day I'd been eagerly anticipating: a full day of fishing on a smaller boat. Unlike the half-day trips, this outing promised fewer passengers, deeper waters, and, hopefully, larger fish. Securing this trip hadn't been easy; I'd booked too late in the season and could only reserve one full-day trip. Lesson learned. Next time, I'll plan further ahead.

I woke up with a mix of excitement and impatience, like a child on Christmas morning. This trip to Alaska, my third, was driven by an insatiable urge to explore its fishing paradise. Alaska is truly the halibut capital of the world, and now I understood why the demand for these trips is so high.

As we prepared to board, I felt the thrill of new possibilities. A new captain, a new crew, and the promise of bigger fish filled me with anticipation. This trip, the culmination of careful planning and spontaneous enthusiasm, was about to begin, and I couldn't wait to see what the day would bring.

About four years ago, I traveled to Alaska hoping to recapture the magic of my first visit 27 years prior. However, the trip turned out to be a significant disappointment. We caught only two salmon over two weeks, and the reason soon became clear: commercial fishermen had blocked the mouth of the river with their nets, preventing fish from migrating upstream. Out of frustration, I drove down to the river's mouth to witness it for myself, and sure enough, the commercial boats were there, nets dropped, catching thousands of pounds of fish while sport fishermen like me struggled. I took pictures to document the situation, disgusted by the imbalance between commercial and recreational fishing. It all boiled down to money and influence, with commercial fishing interests seemingly holding sway over the politicians. The experience left a bitter taste in my mouth, a stark contrast to my incredible memories of Alaska from 1997.

THE CALL TO RETURN

In April 2024, determined to revisit the phenomenal experiences of my earlier Alaskan trips, I planned a return. The memories of my 1997 journey had lingered vividly in my mind—a trip filled with adventure, camaraderie, and plenty of fish. That year, I traveled with three friends, flying into the Kenai on a bush plane to explore remote fishing spots. We caught graylings, trout, and salmon, including my first king salmon, and the awe of that trip stayed with me. This time, I was eager to reclaim those feelings.

When I decided to return, I tried to book full-day fishing trips. Unfortunately, most were already reserved except for one. I settled for several half-day trips instead. As I woke up this morning, the anticipation for my one full-day outing filled me with excitement. Today's trip promised deeper waters and the chance to catch larger halibut, especially as we planned to venture closer to the continental shelf, where the bigger, spawning halibut gather.

MORNING AT HOMER SPIT

The day began early. By 5:30 a.m., we were in the car, driving to Homer Spit. The temperature was in the upper 50s—cloudy but thankfully dry. The Spit, as always, took my breath away. The towering Kenai Mountains stood shrouded in mist, their peaks piercing the clouds like ancient sentinels. It's a view that never fails to mesmerize, and I found myself snapping photos once again, unable to resist capturing the beauty.

We parked near the harbor ramp and made our way down to the floating docks. The tide was mid-level, making the descent manageable. Turning left, we spotted our boat for the day—the *Patriot*. A sleek 30-foot aluminum vessel, it gleamed as if ready to take on the world. Sam, the deckhand, greeted us warmly. Dressed in a bright red waterproof raincoat, he exuded a quiet efficiency. Captain Drew, a soft-spoken man with clean-shaven features and a calm demeanor, soon joined us. He didn't fit the stereotype of a rugged, boisterous sea captain, but his professionalism and warmth quickly earned my respect.

THE JOURNEY OUT

The *Patriot* was smaller than the boats I had been on previously, but it had thoughtful features like rod holders soldered into the railings. These would allow us to rest our rods while waiting for bites—a small detail that made a huge difference in comfort. Inside the cabin, there was a bolted-down table with bench seating for four. There we met our fellow passengers, a family visiting their son and daughter-in-law in Homer. They had come up from Ohio.

From left to right, tall John, Kelly his wife and daughter in law living in Alaska. Scott and Brendale are Mom, Dad from Ohio. Isn't it nice, a family affair.

Captain Drew informed us it would take about two hours to reach the fishing grounds. As we cruised through the Kachemak Bay, Drew shared stories about his life. During the off-season, he worked near the North Pole, placing seismic probes to help locate potential oil fields. The job involved hammering the frozen ground to send vibrations that could reveal underground resources. It was grueling, dangerous work in temperatures as low as -50°F, but it allowed Drew to support his family. His work ethic and resilience were inspiring. Whether managing a team of 50 in the Arctic or captaining a fishing boat in Alaska's waters, Drew epitomized dedication and responsibility.

FISHING AT LAST

We finally arrived at the fishing grounds, anchoring at a depth of 250 feet. The rod holders made it easier to manage the heavier lines needed for such depths. Almost immediately, the action began. Brendale, one of the passengers, caught the first halibut, followed by cod caught by Lauri and John. I, however, stood by patiently, my rod still and unyielding.

The minutes stretched, and my excitement turned to doubt.

Lauri in the early morning bringing in a Halibut.

Everyone else seemed to be reeling in fish after fish, their smiles wide with satisfaction. Then, at last, it happened—a bite! The tip of my rod bent slightly, and I felt the tension in the line. Adrenaline surged as I yanked the rod out of the holder and began reeling furiously. The fish fought hard, and I could feel the weight of its body pulling against me. My arms burned, and I used my whole body to keep the tension on the line.

After what felt like an eternity, I saw the shadow of the fish rising through the water—a massive halibut. Captain Drew and Sam worked together to gaff it and finally hauled it aboard. It thrashed powerfully on the deck, its size taking up nearly the entire cockpit. Drew delivered a quick, humane blow to end its struggle, and I stood there, exhausted but exhilarated. This was the biggest halibut I had ever caught—a true trophy fish

Captain Rami Geffner with a large-size Halibut.

REFLECTIONS

The seas were rough, and our little *Patriot* rocked and rolled as we continued fishing. Despite the conditions, everyone seemed to be in good spirits, except Kelly, who was quietly battling seasickness. She never complained, showing remarkable resilience. I admired her strength; she was tougher than I could have been, under similar circumstances.

The day passed in a blur of activity, laughter, and camaraderie. By the time we returned to the harbor, the tide had shifted, leveling the ramp for an easier walk back to the car. We ended the day with a warm cup of coffee and a sense of accomplishment. This trip was everything I had hoped it would be and even more—a reminder of why Alaska held such a special place in my heart.

As I lay in bed that night, the light from the endless Alaskan summer sky filtering through the curtains, I felt a profound sense of gratitude. The day had been long and exhausting but filled with the kind of joy that only comes from reconnecting with nature and embracing its challenges. This was the Alaska I remembered, the Alaska I loved, and I couldn't wait to see what the next day would bring.

That's why people with seasickness often seek to remain motionless—to minimize the overstimulation of their brains. When the boat starts moving steadily forward, and the rocking and rolling decreases, the brain receives less conflicting information, and the sensation of nausea eases. Today, we were catching significantly more halibut than cod, likely because we had ventured farther out to deeper waters. Yesterday, it seemed the cod outnumbered the halibut. When cod were caught, the crew would immediately chop them up for bait.

Since cod happens to be my favorite fish to eat, I asked the crew to save a few for me to take home. At first, they seemed to ignore my request entirely. When I persisted, asking them to tag and clean a couple of cod for me, their reluctance turned into outright resistance. Frustrated, I pressed them for an explanation. Finally, they claimed that the cod were infested with parasites and unsafe to eat.

As a scientist, their reasoning didn't sit well with me. I knew that parasitic infections in wild fish were common but not unique to cod. Halibut, like cod, are demersal fish that dwell near the seabed and consume similar prey such as crustaceans and mollusks. If cod were a risk, why wouldn't halibut be as well? Their explanation felt like a fabrication. I suspected there were other reasons for their unwillingness to let me keep the cod.

Cod and halibut, like many fish, can carry parasites, but these are typically visible during cleaning and are neutralized by proper cooking. It's a well-known precaution that wild fish should be thoroughly cooked to avoid health risks. Their warnings felt like an excuse to discourage me from keeping the cod.

THE REAL REASONS?

I theorized that their resistance stemmed from practical concerns rather than safety. For one, the boat was advertised as a halibut fishing charter, not a general fishing trip. Most passengers came with the expectation of catching halibut, not cod, and likely had little interest in the latter. Second, if all 25 passengers caught their two-halibut limit and added cod to their haul, the crew would have to clean and fillet significantly more fish. The extra workload wouldn't result in higher tips or pay for the crew, making it an unattractive prospect. By discouraging passengers from keeping cod, the crew reduced their workload and conserved the herring bait for future trips.

Realizing that my efforts to keep cod on this boat were futile, I decided to let it go. Harboring resentment wouldn't help, especially since I had booked several more trips on this charter. From then on, I knew that any cod I caught on the *Spirit* would either be released or chopped up for bait.

A DIFFERENT EXPERIENCE ON THE *PATRIOT*

Today's trip on the *Patriot* offered a stark contrast. When I asked Captain Drew if I could keep a few cod, he responded with a cheerful "No problem." There was no resistance, no fabricated warnings about parasites, and no deaf ears. The cod I brought home that evening were clean and delicious. My suspicions about the *Spirit* crew's motives seemed validated.

The night before, I had researched Alaskan cod and found no

credible warnings against eating them, other than the usual advice to cook fish thoroughly to kill any potential parasites. This applied to all wild fish, including halibut. Cod is a highly regarded fish worldwide, and my experience proved no different.

Meanwhile, Kelly, one of the passengers, quietly battled seasickness throughout the day. She managed to throw up and feel slightly better but never once complained. Her resilience was admirable. Despite her discomfort, she stayed engaged and positive, a true trooper.

A Successful Day

By 2 p.m., we had all reached our limits—two halibut and two cod per person. Sam worked efficiently to clean and fillet the catch, ensuring everything was ready before we reached the dock. The passengers were thrilled, posing for pictures with their fish before we headed back. Even Kelly seemed happier now that the boat was moving steadily forward, her seasickness easing as we approached calmer waters.

The ride back through Kachemak Bay was breathtaking. The Kenai Mountains loomed in the distance, their jagged peaks piercing the low-lying clouds. The landscape was a masterpiece, and the day's successes only added to its beauty. This trip on the *Patriot* felt like a perfect blend of adventure, camaraderie, and respect for the natural world—a reminder of why Alaska holds such a special place in my heart.

The smaller towns along the Kenai Peninsula have been integral to the development of the region, each contributing to its unique history and character. Let's explore the stories of Halibut Cove Lagoon, Sadie Cove, Tutka Bay, and Jakolof

Bay to understand their historical and cultural significance.

HALIBUT COVE LAGOON

Halibut Cove Lagoon, nestled off Kachemak Bay, boasts a rich history deeply intertwined with indigenous cultures and the fishing industry. Before European contact, the Sugpiaq (Alutiiq) people inhabited this area, relying on the lagoon's sheltered waters for fishing and gathering. These activities were vital to their economy and culture, creating a harmonious relationship with the environment.

The arrival of Russian fur traders in the 18th century marked a period of profound change. Trade with the indigenous population introduced new goods but also brought devastating diseases. By the late 19th and early 20th centuries, the region's abundant marine resources attracted settlers, particularly for halibut fishing, which became the cornerstone of the local economy.

In the 20th century, Halibut Cove began to evolve as a destination for tourists drawn by its natural beauty and unique tidal currents. The establishment of Halibut Cove State Park in 1980 further highlighted the area's ecological significance, attracting visitors for kayaking, hiking, and wildlife viewing. Today, the cove is renowned for its picturesque boardwalks and eco-tourism, preserving its serene beauty for residents and travelers alike.

Sadie Cove

Sadie Cove shares a similarly rich history. Before European exploration, the Sugpiaq (Alutiiq) people thrived here, relying on the abundant marine resources of Kachemak Bay. Fishing, hunting, and gathering were integral to their way of life.

The late 18th and early 19th centuries saw the arrival of Russian fur traders, who profoundly impacted the local communities through trade, cultural shifts, and the introduction of diseases. Despite these challenges, the area retained its natural allure, attracting settlers and tourists in the 20th century.

With its dramatic landscapes, rich marine life, and lush forests, Sadie Cove became a haven for outdoor activities such as hiking and kayaking. The inclusion of Sadie Cove within Kachemak Bay State Park in 1980 cemented its role in conservation and eco-tourism. Today, it remains a tranquil escape known for its breathtaking views and recreational opportunities.

Tutka Bay

Tutka Bay, a secluded gem on the southern end of the Kenai Peninsula, offers stunning vistas of mountains, fjords, and glaciers. Before Russian and American settlement, the Alutiiq people lived along its shores, skillfully utilizing the bay's resources for sustenance and cultural practices.

Russian fur traders arrived in the mid-18th century, drawn by the lucrative sea otter pelts. Their presence brought trade opportunities but also conflict and disease, significantly impacting the indigenous population. During the late 19th and early 20th centuries, industries like fishing, logging, and mining flourished nearby, while Tutka Bay itself remained relatively untouched.

The establishment of Kachemak Bay State Park in 1970 marked a turning point for Tutka Bay. As part of Alaska's first state park, the bay became a protected area, ensuring the preservation of its pristine environment. Today, it is a premier destination for eco-tourism, offering activities such as kayaking, fishing, and wildlife observation. Tutka Bay Lodge, known for its sustainable practices, provides luxury accommodations while emphasizing conservation and education.

JAKOLOF BAY

Jakolof Bay, situated west of Tutka Bay, shares its history with nearby Seldovia. Before European contact, the Sugpiaq (Alutiiq) people lived semi-nomadic lives, moving with the seasons and relying heavily on the bay's marine resources.

The Russian era, beginning in the mid-18th century, brought fur traders who sought sea otter pelts. While Seldovia became a hub of Russian-American activity, Jakolof Bay served as a temporary base for hunting expeditions. The introduction of Russian

Orthodox Christianity and the spread of diseases deeply affected the local communities.

The bay experienced a surge of activity during the early 20th century with the discovery of chromite, a mineral vital for producing stainless steel. The Jakolof Bay Chromite Mine operated intermittently, especially during World Wars I and II when demand for strategic minerals spiked. However, as resources dwindled, mining operations declined. Today, remnants of the mining infrastructure serve as historical markers of this industrial period.

Jakolof Bay is now a peaceful retreat, offering fishing, kayaking, and wildlife viewing. It provides a gateway to Kachemak Bay State Park, where visitors can explore trails, glaciers, and diverse ecosystems.

CONCLUSION

These small towns and bays along the Kenai Peninsula reflect the rich interplay between Alaska's indigenous heritage, European colonization, and modern conservation efforts. From the Sugpiaq people's sustainable practices to the industrial booms of chromite mining and halibut fishing, each location tells a story of resilience and adaptation. Today, they stand as testaments to Alaska's natural beauty and cultural significance, drawing visitors from around the world to experience their pristine wilderness and vibrant history.

SELDOVIA, ALASKA: A STORY
OF RESILIENCE AND CHANGE

Seldovia, a charming town on the southern shore of Kachemak Bay, is steeped in history, reflecting the diverse influences of indigenous traditions, Russian colonization, American expansion, and the ebb and flow of the fishing industry. Its story is one of survival, adaptation, and reinvention, shaped by natural beauty and cultural richness.

EARLY HISTORY AND INDIGENOUS ROOTS

For thousands of years, the Sugpiaq (Alutiiq) people lived along the shores of what is now Seldovia. They thrived by mastering the region's abundant marine and land resources, relying on salmon, halibut, seals, sea otters, and a variety of plants for sustenance. Seasonal camps were established, reflecting a deep understanding of the land's rhythms.

The Sugpiaq people developed sophisticated fishing and hunting techniques, crafting tools from bone, wood, and stone. Their semi-nomadic lifestyle allowed them to follow seasonal migrations, ensuring sustainable use of the resources that surrounded them. Seldovia's name is thought to derive from the Russian word *Seldevoy*, meaning "herring bay," acknowledging the area's abundance of herring.

RUSSIAN INFLUENCE

Russian explorers arrived in 1741 under Vitus Bering's leadership, marking the start of Alaska's colonization. Drawn by the lucrative fur trade, particularly sea otter pelts, Russian traders and missionaries established a presence in Seldovia and neighboring areas. Russian Orthodox Christianity took root, blending with local traditions to create a unique cultural heritage.

The Russian era also brought significant challenges. Diseases introduced by the newcomers devastated the Sugpiaq population, reducing their numbers and disrupting their way of life. Despite this, the Alutiiq people adapted, incorporating aspects of Russian culture while maintaining their own.

AMERICAN EXPANSION AND THE RISE OF FISHING

After the United States purchased Alaska in 1867, Seldovia became part of the American frontier. The town's location, nestled along the rich waters of Kachemak Bay, made it a natural hub for commercial fishing. By the late 19th century, settlers and entrepreneurs established fish canneries, transforming Seldovia into a bustling fishing community.

During this time, Seldovia developed its iconic boardwalks, built on wooden pilings to accommodate the tidal flats. These boardwalks connected homes, shops, and businesses, becoming a defining feature of the town's character.

The fishing industry flourished, attracting a diverse population of indigenous people, Russian descendants, and immigrants from Europe and Asia. Seldovia became a vital port and economic center, with salmon, halibut, and herring driving its prosperity.

CHALLENGES AND NATURAL DISASTERS

Seldovia's idyllic existence was forever changed by the 1964 Good Friday Earthquake, one of the most powerful earthquakes in North American history. The land subsided by approximately four feet, leading to widespread flooding during high tides. Much of the original infrastructure, including the iconic boardwalks, was destroyed.

In the aftermath, the town was rebuilt on higher ground, and many of its historic structures were lost. The earthquake marked a turning point for Seldovia, reshaping its physical layout and signaling the decline of its once-thriving fishing industry.

ECONOMIC DECLINE AND REINVENTION

Following the earthquake, Seldovia faced economic challenges. Overfishing, stricter regulations, and competition from larger ports like Homer led to the closure of local canneries. Many residents left in search of opportunities elsewhere, and the town's population dwindled.

In recent decades, however, Seldovia has found new life as a destination for eco-tourism and outdoor recreation. Its stunning landscapes, rich biodiversity, and cultural heritage attract visitors seeking an authentic Alaskan experience. Kayaking, hiking, fishing, and wildlife viewing are now central to the local economy.

CULTURAL PRESERVATION

The Seldovia Village Tribe, representing the area's Alutiiq people, plays a crucial role in preserving the town's heritage. Through cultural programs, health services, and economic initiatives, the tribe ensures that Seldovia's indigenous traditions remain vibrant.

PORT GRAHAM: A NEIGHBOR'S STORY

Just south of Seldovia lies Port Graham, another small village with a rich history. Like Seldovia, it was home to the Sugpiaq people, whose lives centered around the sea. Port Graham shares a similar narrative of Russian influence, American expansion, and reliance on fishing.

Port Graham's remote location has helped preserve its cultural traditions. The Russian Orthodox Church remains a central institution, and the village continues to rely on fishing and subsistence activities, though eco-tourism and cultural programs are becoming increasingly important.

SELDOVIA TODAY

Seldovia stands as a testament to the resilience of its people. While the town no longer relies on fishing as it once did, it has embraced its role as a quiet retreat for those seeking the beauty of Kachemak Bay. Visitors can explore its picturesque harbor, learn about its history, and connect with its vibrant community.

The town's story is a microcosm of Alaska's broader history, reflecting the struggles and triumphs of its indigenous people, the impact of colonization, and the ever-changing tides of economic fortune. Today, Seldovia is not just a place—it's a legacy, a hidden gem offering a glimpse into Alaska's past and present.

In 1883, Saint Augustine Volcano erupted, sending shockwaves through the region. The eruption triggered a massive tidal wave that struck Port Graham, devastating the village and sweeping away their fishing boats. This catastrophic event underscored the vulnerability of the coastal communities in Alaska to natural disasters, leaving a lasting mark on the history of Port Graham.

PORT GRAHAM: FROM SUGPIAQ ROOTS TO MODERN CHALLENGES

Like its neighboring villages, Port Graham's story begins with the Sugpiaq (Alutiiq) people, who lived off the rich marine and terrestrial resources for thousands of years. Their knowledge of the land and sea enabled them to thrive in the harsh environment.

Seasonal fishing, hunting seals, and gathering berries were integral parts of their lives.

RUSSIAN INFLUENCE AND THE FUR TRADE

The arrival of Russian explorers and fur traders in the 18th century marked a significant shift. The Russians sought sea otter pelts, leading to extensive hunting and the establishment of trading posts. During this era, the Russian Orthodox Church became a cornerstone of life in Port Graham. The introduction of Orthodoxy blended with indigenous traditions, creating unique religious and cultural practices still observed today. However, the Russians also brought diseases that decimated the local population.

A VILLAGE OF INDUSTRY

Port Graham was officially recognized as a village in the early 20th century, driven by the growth of the commercial fishing industry. The establishment of the Port Graham Cannery became the economic heartbeat of the community, providing employment and a means to export the abundant fish harvested from nearby waters. Many residents worked as fishermen or in the fish-processing facilities, relying on this industry for their livelihood.

The Alaska Native Claims Settlement Act (ANCSA) of 1971 further shaped Port Graham's future. The creation of the Port Graham Corporation enabled the community to manage land and resources more effectively, representing the interests of its Native shareholders.

THE ROLE OF RUSSIAN ORTHODOXY

The Russian Orthodox Church remains deeply ingrained in Port Graham's identity. A small chapel stands as a symbol of faith and resilience, serving as a gathering place for religious ceremonies, feast days, and cultural celebrations. These events often combine Christian traditions with Sugpiaq practices, showcasing the fusion of two worlds.

MODERN CHALLENGES AND SUBSISTENCE LIVING

By the mid-20th century, changes in the global fishing industry brought economic challenges to Port Graham. Overfishing, environmental changes, and stricter regulations diminished the commercial fishing opportunities that once sustained the village. Today, the community has a population of about 200 people, with many relying on subsistence activities such as hunting, fishing, and gathering to maintain their traditional way of life.

Residents harvest fish, seals, sea lions, and birds, while also gathering berries and other wild resources. These practices are essential not only for sustenance but also for preserving the cultural heritage passed down through generations.

CULTURAL PRESERVATION

Efforts to revitalize the Sugpiaq language and celebrate traditional crafts, music, and food are underway. The Port Graham Corporation and the Native Village of Port Graham tribal government have spearheaded projects aimed at sustainable development and cultural preservation.

RETURNING TO THE HARBOR:
A SNAPSHOT OF HOMER LIFE

After a long day of fishing, we returned to the harbor. The team from the Homer Fish Processing Company was already at the dock, ready to take our catch for processing. They would vacuum-seal and freeze the fish, ensuring it stayed fresh for transport home. As we exited the boat, we tipped the crew and began the arduous climb up the aluminum ramp. With the tide low, the ramp was steep, making the ascent a challenge, especially while carrying heavy bags and wearing clunky boots. Reaching the top of the ramp was a relief. Once there, we swapped our waterproof layers and boots for lighter clothing and sneakers, feeling ready to explore.

Ramp at the Homer Harbor

Exploring Homer Spit

With extra time on our hands, we wandered along the Homer Spit, soaking in the sights. Our first stop was Coal Town Coffee & Tea, where we enjoyed warm, aromatic coffee. From there, we explored **High Tide Arts**, a shop owned by local artist Leslie Klaar. Her work, along with pieces from other Alaskan artists, beautifully captures the natural splendor and wildlife of the region. I bought gifts for my wife and children, including a handmade pocketknife with a caribou antler handle—a small keepsake for myself.

Driving down the Spit.

The shops along the Homer Spit are a testament to the area's creative spirit and connection to nature. Each visit is an opportunity to bring a piece of Alaska's charm home. As the day wound down, I felt a deep appreciation for the blend of history, culture, and natural beauty that defines this unique corner of the world.

The **Coal Town Coffee & Tea**, nestled next to High Tides Arts, is a beloved stop for coffee and tea enthusiasts on the Homer

Spit. The cozy café offers a wide variety of espresso drinks, brewed coffee, specialty teas, and light snacks. Its inviting ambiance is enhanced by breathtaking views of Kachemak Bay, making it a delightful place to recharge while exploring the Spit.

Another gem on the Spit is **Spit Sisters Café**, a family-owned establishment known for its excellent coffee and hearty breakfast and lunch options. A favorite among locals and visitors, the café is perfectly situated near Nomar, a store famous for its rugged outdoor gear, bags, and marine equipment. These two businesses are conveniently located along the main stretch of the Homer Spit Road.

For those who love locally roasted coffee, **K Bay Caffé** offers a seasonal pop-up stand on the Spit. Often set up near busy hubs like the harbor or ferry terminal, this stand serves high-quality espresso drinks, cold brew, and bagged coffee beans for those wanting to savor a piece of Homer at home.

At the base of the Spit, the **Fresh Sourdough Express Bakery & Café** is a must-visit for its legendary baked goods. While primarily known for its sourdough creations, the café also offers a range of coffee and espresso drinks, perfect to pair with a fresh pastry before or after a day of exploring the area.

SHOPS ALONG THE HOMER SPIT

The Homer Spit is bustling with unique shops, offering everything from Alaskan art to fresh seafood. Here are some of the standout spots we visited:

THE SALTY DOG SALOON

- **What They Sell:** Though primarily a bar, this iconic landmark is a must-visit for its atmosphere. The walls are covered in signed dollar bills from patrons, and they sell branded merchandise like T-shirts, hoodies, and hats.
- **Specialty:** Souvenirs and a taste of Homer's history.

COAL POINT TRADING COMPANY

- **What They Sell:** Locally caught seafood, including fresh fish, halibut, and salmon. The shop also features Alaskan gifts like jewelry and clothing.
- **Specialty:** Fresh seafood, smoked salmon, and unique gifts.

NOMAR

- **What They Sell:** High-quality outdoor and marine gear, including durable clothing and custom bags designed for Alaska's rugged conditions.
- **Specialty:** Marine gear and custom outerwear.

CAPTAIN PATTIE'S FISH HOUSE GIFT SHOP

- **What They Sell:** Alaskan-made products, souvenirs, and branded merchandise from the popular restaurant.
- **Specialty:** Local gifts and artisan goods.

HIGH TIDE ARTS

- **What They Sell:** A gallery showcasing local art by Leslie Klaar and other Alaskan artists, featuring paintings, ceramics, prints, and handmade crafts.
- **Specialty:** Alaskan-themed art and ceramics.

HOMER SHORES BOARDWALK

- **What They Sell:** A collection of vendors offering items like locally made jewelry, clothing, art, and crafts.
- **Specialty:** A mix of Alaskan crafts and artwork.

SEAFARER'S MEMORIAL GIFT SHOP

- **What They Sell:** Souvenirs and maritime-themed items, often supporting local causes and the upkeep of the Seafarer's Memorial.
- **Specialty:** Maritime-themed memorabilia.

WASABI'S HOMER SPICE

- **What They Sell:** Locally made spice blends perfect for

seasoning fish and meats. These blends make for unique gifts or a flavorful reminder of Alaska.

- **Specialty:** Alaskan spice blends.

THE FISH FACTORY

- **What They Sell:** A seafood processing service where visitors can ship fresh catch, buy smoked or canned salmon, or process fish they've caught.
- **Specialty:** Fresh and smoked seafood products.

PIER ONE THEATRE GIFT SHOP

- **What They Sell:** Merchandise supporting the local theater, as well as crafts, jewelry, and theater-themed souvenirs.
- **Specialty:** Theater-related gifts and local crafts.

A SATISFYING END TO THE DAY

After exploring the shops and enjoying the vibrant atmosphere of the Spit, it was time to head back for dinner. The drive home was peaceful, filled with anticipation for our evening meal—cod fish tacos paired with brown beans and noodles. It was the perfect ending to a day filled with adventure and discovery.

As we settled in, the thought of tomorrow's plans brought a renewed excitement. The Homer Spit had captivated us with its charm, leaving us eager for what lay ahead in this Alaskan paradise.

CHAPTER 16

JULY 27

A Morning on the *Foxfire*

The morning began at 6:30 a.m., sipping coffee while catching up on the latest news. Soon, it was time to leave. We packed up our layers of clothing and Boggs boots, loading them into the car for another fishing adventure. Our drive started on Homer's Main Street, heading south onto the Sterling Highway (AK-1). Passing Beluga Lake, we crossed over to Homer's mainland and drove into the Spit.

Today, we were headed to a new vessel—the *Foxfire*—contracted by Rainbow Tours for morning trips. The *Foxfire*, slightly smaller than the *Spirit*, accommodated 23 passengers and departed at 7:00 a.m. sharp, returning by 3:00 p.m. It traveled roughly 25 miles out from Homer Harbor, much like the *Spirit*, but handled the morning routes.

The *Foxfire*'s crew included Captain Grant, James, and Luke. Grant, with his long, curly hair and medium beard, gave off a relaxed vibe, though his demeanor was more serious than commanding. James, on the other hand, exuded warmth and enthusiasm. He was the kind of crew member who knew everyone's name by the end of the trip and was always there when you needed him. As it turned out, James also owned a restaurant in Homer, serving dinner in the evenings. Luke, the second crew member, was a lanky young man with a patchy beard and boyish charm. Timid and soft-spoken, he was easy to overlook unless you were specifically looking for him.

Into Kachemak Bay

Once everyone was aboard, zip ties were distributed for tagging our catches. We set off from Homer Harbor, turning starboard into the Alaska Marine Highway through Kachemak Bay. This 40-mile-long bay, divided into north and south sections relative to the Spit, has a rich history. The name "Kachemak" originates from the Alutiiq word meaning "Smokey Bay," a nod to the coal steams that once smoldered along the bay.

As we navigated the bay, we eventually reached the Gulf of Alaska, zigzagging to locate fish on the sounder. By 9:00 a.m., we dropped anchor at a depth of 200 feet. The sea was calm and the sky sunny. The temperature climbed from the upper 40s to around 60. With minimal current, a two-pound sinker was sufficient to drop our bait to the ocean floor.

Fishing Frenzy

The action was immediate. As soon as the bait hit the seabed, bites were felt across the boat. A flurry of halibut reeled in from every corner sent the crew—Grant, James, and Luke—scurrying to assist. Whether it was unhooking fish, rebaiting lines, or hauling halibut over the rails, the crew worked tirelessly. Even Captain Grant emerged from the flybridge to lend a hand.

John Devine with his son Will, enjoying the peace and serenity of fishing on the Foxfire They came from California. Then James the first mate helped Lauri. The stern of the boat held a lot of fishing poles. The price of the day were the Halibuts we caught. The lower picture shows the inside of the Foxfire.

The fish kept coming, and with each catch, the excitement on board grew. High-fives were exchanged, and laughter echoed across the deck. However, lifting 25-pound fish from the waterline to the rail, about 10 feet, quickly became exhausting. Many passengers, including myself, reached their bag limit early. Having caught my two halibut, I set my rod aside and leaned against a post, enjoying the spectacle and observing the catches being brought aboard.

In the distance, the clear day offered breathtaking views. To the bow, I spotted what I was certain was Kodiak Island, and to starboard, the majestic chain of mountains—likely Mount Augustine, Mount Iliamna, and Mount Redoubt—stood tall against the horizon.

THE VOLCANIC GIANTS

The nearby volcanoes, part of the Aleutian volcanic arc, are a reminder of the dynamic forces shaping this region. Their history is deeply intertwined with the area's geology and culture.

Mount Augustine (75 miles southwest of Homer)

- Known for its explosive eruptions, including one in 1883 that caused a tsunami affecting Port Graham.

- Location: Augustine Island, southwest of Homer in Cook Inlet.

- Other major eruptions in 1935, 1963–64, 1976, 1986, and 2006 left ashfall over the Kenai Peninsula and disrupted life in nearby villages.

Mount Redoubt (110 miles from Homer)

- Infamous for its 1989–90 eruption, which grounded a Boeing 747 in an ash cloud. Villages like Homer experienced ashfall that disrupted fishing and travel. Location: On the western side of Cook Inlet, northwest of Homer.

Mount Iliamna (135 miles southwest of Homer)

- Though less active, Iliamna's fumaroles and seismic activity serve as a reminder of its potential.

- Location: Southwest of Mount Redoubt, also on the western side of Cook Inlet.

The Power of Pyroclastic Flows

As I thought about the deadly pyroclastic flows—hot, fast-moving clouds of ash, gas, and rock fragments capable of incinerating anything in their path. The 1964 Good Friday Earthquake, which coincided with Mount Augustine's eruption, brought these dangers to the forefront, devastating communities like Seldovia and Port Graham.

HEADING BACK AND WRAPPING UP THE DAY

Everyone on board eventually caught their bag limit, and we returned to Homer Harbor earlier than expected. As usual, the Homer Fish Processing Company was there to collect the freshly caught fillets. By 3:30 p.m., we were walking up the steep aluminum ramp to the marina, now at a 45-degree angle due to the low tide.

A SCENIC DRIVE

Around 4 p.m., we left the Spit and decided to take a scenic drive along Homer's East End Road, which winds along Kachemak Bay. The views were stunning. I sat in the back seat, taking pictures and videos of the breathtaking landscapes, including fields of pink fireweed, cow parsnip, yarrow, bluish-purple irises, and junipers. The kaleidoscope of colors was incredible.

DINNER AND A HEALTH TIP

As the day wound down, we opted for an early dinner. As a physician, I always advocate for eating earlier to avoid nocturnal regurgitation, which can lead to serious health risks such as aspiration pneumonia and esophageal damage.

For dinner, we enjoyed stuffed green, yellow, and red peppers with rice and halibut. We used a Cosori air fryer, a versatile and easy-to-use appliance we'd discovered during our stay at the Airbnb. The Cosori not only fries but also roasts, broils, and bakes. Lightweight, compact, and easy to clean, it's perfect for home or travel. I'm already planning to purchase one for my house and boat when I return home.

The day had been another memorable one in Homer, filled with great fishing, stunning scenery, and delicious food.

CHAPTER 17

JULY 28-29

ROUTINE AND RECORD CATCHES

Over the next two days, we fell into a familiar, comforting rhythm. Mornings began with hot coffee and the news, our quiet prelude to whatever the day might hold. We layered up, grabbed our Boggs boots, and headed to the Homer Spit, soaking in its staggering beauty anew each morning. No matter how many times you see it, the Spit feels like the most stunning place on Earth—it never gets old..

Both days, we climbed aboard the *Foxfire* with Captain Grant and his crew, James and Luke. The waters were calm, and luck was on our side: we hit our halibut bag limit before 11:00 AM. By early afternoon, we were back in the harbor, our catch tucked away and the rest of the day wide open.

Evenings were laid-back and content. Good food, good stories, and the quiet kind of joy that comes from being somewhere beautiful, doing something you love. Each day felt full, and just the right kind of simple.

Beluga Bay

CHAPTER 18

JULY 30

AN EARLY START AND MORE DISCOVERIES

We started our drive early this morning to avoid rushing to reach the *Foxfire* on time and running down the floating dock in fear of missing its departure. The day was calm, and the sun was shining. There were a few clouds in the sky, and the peaks of the Kenai Mountains gleamed like beads of pearls.

We boarded the *Foxfire*, and once everyone was on the boat, we headed out to sea.

As we arrived at the fishing grounds, we could see traces of the volcanic mountains and Kodiak Island in the distance. I thought of Mount Augustine, an active volcano that had caused havoc in the past. Captain Grant did an excellent job navigating us to the fishing grounds. Since the waters were calm, he decided to anchor the boat in 200 feet of water. Anchoring was the best choice for catching fish because the chum used to attract the fish stays around the boat, bringing the fish closer.

Without any issues, we lowered our sinkers to the ocean floor, where the demersal fish were waiting. The boat was packed with passengers from all over, many of whom had likely decided to fish in Homer as an afterthought. This could explain why so many people get seasick—they haven't had the chance to acclimate their bodies to the rocking and rolling of a boat at sea.

I remembered my early fishing days, going out on research vessels and experiencing dreadful seasickness. Despite the nausea, I kept going back until my body acclimated to the motion of the ocean. Even now, if I spend too much time away from the sea, I need a short period to reacclimate before I feel completely comfortable again. Knowing this process is half the battle, now I'm one of the few people who can go out in rough seas without issue.

Kenai Mountains, East of Homer

Unfortunately, many passengers don't have this advantage. Feeling good on vacation and knowing Homer is the world's halibut capital often inspires them to try fishing. However, a significant number of them end up seasick.

HALIBUT AND THEIR FASCINATING LIFE CYCLE

Halibut have a fascinating life cycle and migratory patterns, which contribute to their plentiful numbers. The government has implemented effective legislation to limit the size and number of fish that can be caught and bagged, ensuring sustainability.

KEY FACTS ABOUT PACIFIC HALIBUT

The Pacific Halibut is found on the continental shelf of North America, the Bering Sea and in the Gulf of Alaska. It is fished by commercial, sport, and subsistence fishers.

Halibut are demersal, living near the ocean floor in temperatures ranging from 37°F to 46°F. Mature halibut gather on spawning grounds along the edge of the continental shelf from November to March, at depths of 600–1,500 feet.

Halibut are strong swimmers and are able to migrate long distances. Halibut of all ages and sizes predominantly migrate clockwise (northwest to southeast) from their settlement areas (western part of the Gulf of Alaska and Bering Sea). Reproductive fish also make regular seasonal migrations from shallow feeding grounds in summer to deeper spawning grounds in winter.

The Gulf of Alaska and the Bering Sea are separated by the Aleutian Islands.

Pacific halibut have diamond-shaped bodies, more elongated than most flatfish, with a width about one-third of their length. They have a high arch in the lateral line over the pectoral fin and a lunate, crescent-shaped tail, distinct from other flatfish. Small scales are embedded in their skin. Halibut have both eyes on their dark upper side, which varies in coloration to match the ocean bottom, allowing them to avoid detection by prey and predators. Their lighter underside appears more like the sand below.

These large flatfish can weigh up to 500 pounds and grow over eight feet long. They are strong swimmers, eating a variety of fish, including cod, turbot, and pollock, as well as invertebrates like octopus, crab, and shrimp. Sometimes, they leave the ocean bottom to feed on pelagic fish such as salmon and herring.

Halibut begin life as larvae in an upright position, with an eye on each side of their head. As they grow, their left eye migrates to the right side, and they assume the flatfish form. Females mature at 8–12 years and lay 0.5–4 million eggs annually, depending on their size. Young halibut float with ocean currents before settling on shallow nursery grounds like the Bering Sea.

The fertilization process of halibut in Alaska is external, meaning that eggs and sperm are released into the water column where fertilization takes place. Here's how the process works:

1. SPAWNING BEHAVIOR:

- **Timing and Location:** During the winter spawning season (November to March), mature male and female halibut migrate to deep waters, typically ranging from 600 to 1,500 feet, near the continental shelf edges in the Gulf of Alaska.

- **Group Spawning:** Halibut may gather in groups at these deep-water spawning grounds.

2. EGG AND SPERM RELEASE:

- **Females:** A single female can produce millions of eggs (up to four million, depending on her size and age). These eggs are released into the water column during spawning.

- **Males:** Males release sperm (milt) into the water simultaneously with the females.

3. FERTILIZATION:

- **External Process:** The eggs and sperm meet in the surrounding water. Sperm swim toward the eggs, and when a sperm cell penetrates an egg, fertilization occurs.
- **Environmental Factors:** Fertilization success depends on factors such as water temperature, currents, and proximity of males and females during spawning.

4. EGG DEVELOPMENT:

- **Buoyancy:** Fertilized eggs are slightly buoyant and float upward in the water column.
- **Incubation:** The eggs develop over a few weeks, during which time they are carried by ocean currents.

5. LARVAL STAGE:

- The fertilized eggs hatch into larvae, which remain planktonic for several months.
- Larvae drift with currents, eventually settling in shallower coastal or shelf areas, where they develop into juvenile halibut.

This reproductive strategy allows for the dispersal of halibut offspring across a wide area, increasing the chances of survival and colonization in suitable habitats.

OUR FISHING TRIP

With the fish bag limit reached, we headed back to the dock, arriving at around 1 p.m. It had been a great trip—the seas were calm, the sun was shining, and plenty of fish were caught.

After returning, it was time to explore the shops on the Homer Spit. I wanted to find some gifts for my family, as I missed them and was always thinking of them.

HIGH TIDE ARTS

One of my favorite stores on the Spit was High Tide Arts, featuring beautiful artwork by Leslie Klaar. Her acrylic paintings focused on the natural and native beauty of Alaska. Her perspectives, simplicity, and sharpness gave her work a peaceful, easy quality that resonated with me.

High Tide's Artwork

The shop also had stunning turquoise and blue native jewelry, as well as stones crafted into bracelets and necklaces. I especially loved the pocketknives carved from shed moose antlers (no animals were harmed, as these antlers are naturally shed).

I ended up buying a couple of the knives and a few pieces of jewelry—perfect keepsakes from my time in Homer.

DINNER AND REFLECTION

Dinner that evening was a feast: Teriyaki halibut, baked potatoes, beans, and a crisp green salad. We also prepared lox from a fillet of sockeye salmon we had caught earlier. Packed in salt and sugar and vacuum-sealed, the salmon was set to marinate for a few days, promising a flavorful treat.

As the day wound down, exhaustion crept in. By 8:30 p.m., I was ready to close my eyes, grateful for the experiences and memories of the day. Tomorrow, being Wednesday, would be a non-fishing day due to regulations. While I would miss being out on the water, it was an opportunity to explore Homer further—a chance to uncover new adventures in this extraordinary place.

CHAPTER 19

JULY 31

It's Wednesday, and there will be no halibut fishing today, according to the rules and regulations of the Alaska government. That is a good thing—one day per week dedicated to conservation for the halibut. Most halibut fishing occurs during the summer when the halibut are closer to shore. By November, they begin their migration from these shallow waters to deeper ones in order to spawn. During the winter months, after spawning, their larvae drift back to the shallower water where they can mature before they themselves are ready to return to the depths of the sea to carry on their own cycle.

AirBnB

I didn't want to waste any time, as we would be leaving soon, and this would be the only full day remaining to explore the area further. After a hearty breakfast, we walked out of the house. As we opened the front door, we saw two little rabbits, one brown and one black, grazing in the front yard. They seemed friendly, and although wild, they had attempted to get close to me once before. However, upon sensing my human scent, they ran away.

In Homer, Alaska, rabbits graze on a variety of plants depending on the season and availability:

IN THE SPRING AND SUMMER:

- **Grasses:** Wild grasses like bluegrass and fescue are staples for rabbits.
- **Herbs and weeds:** Clover, dandelions, plantain, and other wild herbs are favored.
- **Vegetation:** Tender shoots, leaves, and stems of plants.
- **Garden plants:** If they have access to gardens, rabbits may nibble on lettuce, kale, and carrots.
- **Wildflowers:** Many wildflowers, like fireweed, are consumed by rabbits in the summer.

IN THE FALL:

- **Leaves:** Fallen leaves from trees and shrubs.

- **Woody plants:** Tender bark and twigs from bushes like willow and alder.

IN THE WINTER:

- **Bark and twigs:** With limited green vegetation available, rabbits turn to the bark and twigs of woody plants such as willow, birch, and alder.
- **Stored food:** If near humans, they might eat hay or leftover garden materials if available.

Rabbits in Homer thrive on a mix of native plants, adapting to seasonal changes. I took plenty of pictures of the rabbits and then hopped into the SUV.

Our first trip of the day began with a visit to the Center for Alaskan Coastal Studies. I anticipated seeing a lot of educational material. The staff was very nice, but I felt the building was more for community interactions than for didactic learning. They had brochures offering tours of Homer and a gift shop-like area. It was a very confusing place for me. However, I did purchase posters of Alaskan berries and wildflowers. I liked these posters because, besides being great souvenirs, they would also come in handy for my paintings and general knowledge. I also wanted to contribute to Homer's economy. I take this seriously because I am crazy about

Alaska. Remember, it's my third trip here, and I hope to visit more often.

Coastal Center

Driving further into town, we came across an incredibly impressive stone-brick building that looked like a bastion, at least from the side of the parking lot. It stood out like a sore thumb off the Sterling Highway, with a long, wide concrete walkway sitting against the backdrop of the Kenai Mountains and Kachemak Bay. The panoramic view from the back of the building was spectacular and mesmerizing.

The entrance to the visitor center took us through thick, heavy glass doors encased in metal frames. This was just the beginning, and I knew it spoke to us of strength and history.

Inside, the first object we saw was a life-sized replica of a dory—a flat-bottomed boat with a V-shaped bow resembling a large rowboat with bench seats and oars. A modern version of the dory showed an outboard engine mounted on the stern. A plaque nearby explained that biologists used such boats in both the best and worst weather to ferry precious food and equipment to camps on the isolated islands of the Alaska Maritime National Wildlife Refuge.

As we walked further, the building opened into a huge atrium, which transitioned into an even larger atrium with high ceilings. Floor-to-ceiling windows provided a magnificent view of Kachemak Bay and the Kenai Mountains—an incredible backyard vista for this space.

The exhibits were fascinating, offering insights into Alaska's maritime history, wildlife, and indigenous cultures.

This atrium housed several exhibits, including a life-sized statue of a sea lion. At first, I thought it might be a walrus, but the lack of tusks confirmed it was a sea lion. A nearby plaque described the difference: While both are large marine mammals, walruses use their tusks to forage for mussels and clams on the ocean floor, pulling them onto ice to eat. Their tusks, which are large canine teeth, grow throughout their lives and can reach over three feet in length.

As we walked through the museum we began to understand the story of what had happened in this area of Alaska many years ago. It started with presenting "High Rise Groceries," which was one of the first displays on a plaque at the museum as we passed through. It stated that for the first people, the wilderness provided a bounty of fresh delicacies and useful materials. In the long days of summer, freshly laid gull and murre eggs were gathered by young boys scaling cliffs. Birds were hunted by the Inupiat and Yupik people using bolas and nets. The skin of 40 tufted puffins or 25 cormorants were sewn together by the Unanagan people of the Aleutian Islands to make a single, elaborate, full-reversible parka.

The Unangans gave the seasons names that echoed their way of life. In February they named the moon where the last of food would be stored. The March moon would be for eating skin. April represented the near-hunger moon, and May was the moon of flowers, sea pups, and the hunter paddler. June was described as the moon of eggs and seal yearlings, and July was the moon of red fish (salmon) and young seals. August's moon was when grass was fading. September's moon was when one would have to store food and ration it.

The part on the land and sea talked about how the coastal people's understanding of the ocean— including currents and tides, wind and skin, and changing seasons—allowed the Aleuts to expertly navigated their baidarkas through turbulent waters and prevalent dense fog surrounding many islands.

Native people traveled from place to place in search of food resources that also moved and changed seasonally. They located their villages near cliffs, bays, reefs, and islets where they would have the greatest access to marine foods and materials for shelter and clothing. Although local wildlife fluctuated based on hunting patterns, people and animals lived in balance in this marine environment for millennia.

There were illustrations showing how the Natives who lived there understood the ocean's currents and tides. They knew the wind in the sky. In the changing seasons, the elite expertly navigated their boats through turbulent waters and traveled from place to place within this area in search of food.

As we continued our journey through the museum, there were lifelike wooden and clay decoys of the different types of ducks that lived in this area including the surf scoter, common merganser, sea duck, Barrow's goldeneye, hooded merganser, Labrador duck, long-tailed oldsquaw, black scoter, bufflehead, and Harlequin duck.

The Rush Begins

Survivors of the Bering Expedition sparked a "fur rush" in 1742 when they returned to Russia with sea otter pelts from Alaska's coast. To the sailors' amazement, a single pelt in the Chinese market was worth three times their yearly pay.

The fur rush would last 170 years and decimate populations of Native peoples and native animals. Approximately 15,000 Unangans lived in the Aleutians when the Russians arrived. Disease, combined with forced labor and social upheaval, would reduce their numbers to around 2,000 by 1831.

As I kept walking, after having personally seen sea otters in the ocean on the way to the fishing grounds, I was even more heartbroken for these adorable animals. I now came to the sea otter slaughter exhibit. Back then people were lacking all sorts of things that we take for granted. They were trying to survive, needing food, clothes, and shelter. They came to achieve those necessities by trading sea otter furs for money by sacrificing the animals. Money and greed were the driving force at the expense of animals who lived in nature, but that is the way it used to be.

One of the plaques talked about the Russian fur traders, who pushed through the Aleutians, the Kodiak Archipelago, and on to southeast Alaska, subjugating the Native people to hunt for sea otters for them. By 1860, not only Russian but also British, French, Spanish, and American fur traders had harvested approximately 600,000 sea otters on the southeast coast. By 1899, sea otters were so rare that none of the scientists on the Harriman Alaska expedition reported seeing even one. It so happens that sea otters have the densest fur of all animals, with 650,000 hairs per square inch. Since they kept people extremely warm and plush, they were one of the most highly priced furs.

As I walked a few more feet, they talked about the sea otter slaughter in detail. They had an example of one of these sea otter furs on the wall and invited us to touch it and see what it felt like. I touched it and realized how thick indeed it was. I would never have imagined had I not done that. It was incredible how dense the fur was.

The next plaque at the museum dealt with the rush for hunting furs. Survivors of the Bering expedition sparked a rush for furs in 1742. When they returned to Russia with otter pellets, a single pelt on the Chinese market was worth three times their yearly pay. The fur rush lasted for 170 years and decimated populations of Native people and the animals. Approximately 15,000 Unangans lived in the Aleutians when the Russians arrived, but disease combined with forced labor and social upheaval reduced their numbers to around 2000 by 1831. Within 90 years, 90 percent of the population was wiped out. That was horrible.

The story continued with pockets of hope. By the mid-1800s, the Russians recognized they could not continue to deplete marine resources without ruining the fur industry. But this awareness came too late to save overhunted Steller's sea cows and flightless spectacled cormorants from extinction. Now probably in shame and alarmed, the Russians created a sea otter refuge on Amchitka Island by removing all people and prohibited hunting on the island's shallow nearshore reefs, which became a safe feeding area to help the otters repopulate. Amchitka was one of the several havens for the Aleutians for sea otters, providing hope for their recovery.

It appears that sea otters were not the only marine life that was compromised by early invaders of the islands. More than 200 years ago, Russian fur traders resettled Unangan hunters on the uninhabited Pribilof Islands as laborers for fur seal harvest. In 1867 the United States purchased Alaska, gaining control of this lucrative industry. Its profits recouped the territory's purchase price in only a few years. Hunters continued to harvest valuable northern fur seals for American traders until 1985. Today, more than two-thirds of the world's northern fur seals breed on these islands.

There was also a craving to get fox furs around the same time. In the late 1700s Russian fur traders began transplanting pairs of foxes onto the Aleutian Islands as seed for a new crop of furs. Following the United States' purchase of Alaska in 1867, American fox farmers expanded their fox breeding operations for fur production to at least 45 islands. Many Alaska Natives earned good income trapping foxes until the fur market crashed in the Great Depression of the 1930s. Trapping tapered off in the 1940s, but the foxes remained.

A Russian wrote that "foxes have chased off the fowl, which nowadays are afraid even to come ashore." Another report added that where there were no foxes, there were many birds. Ground squirrels and voles were even introduced to some islands to feed the foxes after they had eaten most of the birds.

The Aleutian Islands Reservation was created in 1913 to protect both seabirds and fur farming. But by the 1930s biologists recognized that the reservation's dual purpose was a major folly as birds declined or disappeared on many Fox Islands. In 1941 the refuge took its first steps to address the problem, revoking leases on 14 percent of the islands.

As I walked down the hallway after reading the presentations on the slaughter of the otters, seals, foxes, puffins, and other species, I could not help but wonder more about the earlier history of Alaska. Who first settled the area? Where did they come from? And other thoughts.

The history of Alaska dates back to the Upper Paleolithic Period (around 14,000 BC), when foraging groups crossed the Bering Land Bridge into what is now western Alaska. At the time of European contact by the Russian explorers, the area was populated by Alaska Native groups. The name "Alaska" derives from the Aleut word *Alaxsxaq* (also spelled *Alyeska*), meaning "mainland" (literally, "the object toward which the action of the sea is directed").

The US purchased Alaska from Russia in 1867. In the 1890s, gold rushes in Alaska and the nearby Yukon Territory brought thousands of miners and settlers to Alaska. Alaska was granted territorial status in 1912 by the United States of America.

In 1942, two of the outer Aleutian Islands—Attu and Kiska—were occupied by the Japanese during World War II, and their recovery for the US became a matter of national pride. The construction of military bases contributed to the population of Alaska, which was granted US statehood on January 3, 1959.

In 1964, the massive "Good Friday earthquake" killed 131 people and leveled several villages.

The 1968 discovery of oil at Prudhoe Bay and the 1977

completion of the Trans-Alaska Pipeline led to an oil boom.

In 1989 the *Exxon Valdez* hit a reef in Prince William Sound, spilling between 11 and 34 million US gallons (42,000 and 129,000 cubic meters) of crude oil over 1,100 miles (1,800 kilometers) of coastline.

Today, the battle between philosophies of development and conservation is seen in the contentious debate over oil drilling in the Arctic National Wildlife Refuge.

There was a wall of plaques highlighting additional facts about the history of Alaska.

- In 1741, Vilus Bering, for whom the Bering Sea is named, with Georg Wilhelm the naturalist, noted species of wildlife previously unknown to Western science.

- In 1745 the first wave of Russians landed on the Aleutian Islands, forcing the Aleut to hunt sea otters.

- In 1750 Russian traders introduced foxes to feast on abundant seabirds.

- In 1768, the 25-foot-long Steller's sea cow was wiped out through overhunting by Russian mariners. A mere 27 years after the Steller's sea cow had been discovered by the Bering expedition and 100 years later, the flightless spectacled cormorant was eliminated.

- In 1778 Captain James Cook explored Alaska's coastline as far as the Bering Strait in search of an elusive Northwest passage. This is the passage now between Russia and the United States that is present between the Bering Sea to the south and the Chukchi Sea north. Cook Inlet is named after him.

- In 1780 a shipwreck on an Aleutian island introduced rats to the island, which was worse than the oil spills because rats crawl into nesting burrows.

- From 1786 to 1787 Gavil Pribilof, for whom the Pribilof Islands are named after sadly enough, discovered the pupping grounds of millions of northern fur seals, on a pair of islands isolated in the Bering Sea. Wanting to cash in on new riches, Gavil Pribilof relocated 137 Aleuts from Atka and Unalaska and forced them to harvest the furs from the seals. This was the beginning of nearly two centuries of servitude for these Alaska Natives.

- In 1796 an underwater volcano in the eastern Aleutians caused the formation of a new island named Bogoslof.

- Beginning in 1798 Russian fur traders exported a total of more than 400,000 fur seals, 96,000 sea otter furs, and 102,000 fox pelts from Pribilof, Aleutian, and Kodiak islands.

- In 1824 Russia allowed Americans and British to trade in Alaska. The Russian Orthodox Church set up missions on the Aleutians to convert the Aleuts.

- In 1843 Bowhead whales were hunted in the North Pacific and the Arctic waters, and within the next few years 500 New England whale fishing boats slaughtered them. By 1852, 2,682 of these whales were killed, and by 1855 they were reduced to extinction.

- In 1869 Congress created the Pirbilof Islands preservation to protect the fur seals in Alaska.

- In 1881 after more than a century, the Unganan population was reduced to only two settlements.

- In 1892 President Harrison declared a fish, cultural, and forest reserve to be managed by the Alaska Maritime National Wildlife Refuge at Afognak Island.

- In 1898–99 America through the works of noted nature writers and artists got a glimpse of the beauty of Alaska for the first time.

- In 1900 the Lacey Law was passed to protect and safeguard wildlife for the new century in Alaska.

- In 1903 through President Theodore Roosevelt, the National Wildlife Refuge System was born, protecting 93 million acres.

- In 1909 the protection of other territories in Alaska expanded, to be overseen by the Maritime National Wildlife Refuge.

- In 1911, the International Treaty for the Protection and

Preservation of Fur Seals was born...but they would still be hunted until 1985.

- In 1912–13 President Taft added protection and preservation for birds in the Aleutian area.

- In 1918 Congress passed the Protection of Migratory Birds Act.

- From 1930 to 1932 President Hoover created more wildlife refuges.

- From 1932 to 1938 biologists condemned the decision to having allowed fox farming.

- In 1942 Japan invaded the islands of Attu and Kiska in the Aleutian Islands.

- In 1945 the US fortified its commitment to the defense of Alaska.

- In 1949 foxes were removed from the refuge.

- In 1956 comprehensive reform was passed that established the fish and wildlife services to manage the refuges.

- In 1959 Alaska incorporated as the 49th state of the USA.

- In 1962–63, 300 Aleutian Canadian geese were discovered on Buldir Island.

- From 1965 to 1971 underwater nuclear tests were conducted.

- In 1973 Aleutian Canadian geese were declared

endangered.

- In 1976 the Aleutian Islands were designated a UNESCO biosphere reserve.

- In 1980 President Carter signed the Alaska National Interest Lands Conservation Act, which led to 4.9 million acres of seabird refuge.

- In 1982–85 the Pribilof Islands were purchased by the US from the Local Village Corporations.

- In 1987 the 120-foot M/V Tiglax ship (*Tiglax* means "eagle" in Unangan) was commissioned to work with the Maritime National Wildlife Refuge. It had six crew and could carry 16 passengers. Home port was Homer, and the most distant Aleutian Island was 1,500 miles away. It was a twin-diesel boat coursing at 10 knots. This ship was a lifeline to field crews. It was the only transportation to remote island field camps, bringing supplies and biologists and getting all home safely in the fall.

- In 1989 the *Exxon Valdez* oil tanker spilled 10.8 million barrels of oil, equivalent to 125 Olympic-sized swimming pools. The spill's destruction reached 250 miles away. The Exxon Valdez Oil Spill Trustee Council was formed.

- In 2001 the Aleutian Canadian geese were removed from the endangered list.

In the summer months, 40 million seabirds live in colossal colonies located on the islands and headlands of the Alaska Maritime National Wildlife Refuge. More seabirds live in this refuge than in all the rest of North America. It's all about location, location, location. They do so for good fishing and safety from land predators. Each year, refuge biologists return to monitoring sites where they observe and carefully record information to detect anything unusual. At each site field crews count breeding birds, record nesting dates, count the number of eggs and chicks produced, and monitor chick growth and survival. By comparing annual records, biologists know whether the birds nested early or late and how many nested compared to other years. They can identify population trends and spot troubling changes. They may even discover clues that can reveal the cause of the problem. Asking the questions is the first step toward solving the problems.

From the Southeast to the Arctic, field crews are busy checking what parent birds are feeding their chicks. This gives them clues about the quantity and type of food available. Biologists observe seabirds that sample different parts of the marine food web by feeding in four different ways: surface fish eaters, surface plankton eaters, diving fish eaters, and diving plankton eaters. Sometimes the diving birds find plenty to eat and the surface feeders do not, or the plankton eaters may do well but not the fish eaters. Not relying completely on these bird observations, field crews also troll for invertebrates and fish to further investigate the status of the food sources. But comparing data collected at monitoring sites around the refugees can contribute to a bigger picture of the ocean's health.

The scientists who work at the wildlife refuge monitor seabirds and work with other scientists from universities and government agencies, Native communities, and international groups. The refuge and its partners return islands to native ground-nesting birds by removing introduced foxes, reindeer, and feral cattle. They prevent the introduction of bird-killing rats to the refugee island, they clean up contaminants on islands, and they restore habitats. They also identify protected species, unique to the refuge islands such as the Pribilof rock, sandpiper, Aleutian shield fern, and Amack tundra vole. They look for ways to help troubled species such as the endangered Steller sea lions, threatened Stele eiders, declining sea otters, and harlequin ducks.

At the visitor center, I learned that after 45 years, refuge lands again provided the closest basis to the new enemy—the Soviet union. Seabirds and sea otters shared islands with top security, radar, and communication sites on Attu, Shemya, Amchitka, Adak, and Cape Lisburn. The Adak naval base facility grew into the fifth largest city in Alaska before relations with Russia warmed, then the base was shut down in 1997.

There was also information at the visitor center that

discussed the three nuclear bombs detonated under Amchitka Island from 1965 to 1971, to verify the military's ability to detect Soviet underground testing. When Cannikin, the third largest nuclear bomb, exploded, the land violently heaved, water rushed from a wetland, and rocks rained into the ocean. Many marine birds, animals, and fish on and around the island died in the brief but powerful blast. Much had been learned about how the earth moves and cracks in this seismically active region. Fears linger that the earth movements may have allowed radioactive residue to leak into the environment. Long-term monitoring will be essential for understanding the ramifications of these entombed radioactive materials.

Troop ships and landing crafts brought permanent invaders. Norway rats hitchhiked on early merchant ships to Dutch Harbor, Rat Island, and a handful of other islands. During World War II, they spread to many islands with military bases. The problem with these rats is that they prey on eggs, chicks, and small birds, especially those birds that build their nests on the ground and burrow. This scourge falls to the capital refuge to protect and secure against these rats.

There was a shift in the direction taken when biologists began to appreciate the threats that foxes, reindeer, cattle, and other introduced animals posed to the native wildlife. It was said that in 1937, Murie, a biologist with the refuge, warned of the extinction of the Aleutian Canadian geese. These geese, like many other birds, were declining because of the fox predation. Recognizing the conflict between seabirds and foxes was the start. After World War II, the refuge started to place priority on protecting wildlife over commercial interests. Today wildlife continues to come first.

I learned something about the shape of a bird's egg. Murres, for instance, lay their eggs on high, narrow rock ledges of cliffs without any protection of a nest. Some people think that this pear-shaped egg that they lay is an adaptation that helps the egg stay on the bare rock and not roll overboard. Pear-shaped eggs tend to roll in an arc instead of rolling straight off the cliff edge. However, other biologists think that this pear shape has nothing to do with keeping the egg on the cliff, but instead allows more of the surface of the egg to have greater contact with the warm brood patch on the parent's breast. So it appears to be controversial.

At the visitor center I learned that the big Laysan albatross visits Alaska each summer. These birds usually remain far out at sea, gliding over the waves at speeds up to 40 mph, which is fast. Their bodies are small in comparison to their long, narrow wings, which is similar to a glider of a plane that rides the wind. Like most seabirds, the albatross's survival strategy is to lay only one egg per year, invest more time in each chick, and live longer. They tend to live for 35 years.

Small birds, such as the least auklet, fly with rapid wing beats and form huge swirling swarms. These seabirds nest in talus slopes and beach boulders in enormous colonies on islands in the Bering Sea and the Aleutians, which are slopes of small, loose rocks that have fallen from bigger ones above them. The birds also rest on boulders in enormous colonies. The least auklet weighs only about three ounces, which is about the same weight as a sparrow. They fly each summer to Saint Lawrence Island and the Pribilof Islands to reunite with others.

The other birds of Kachemak Bay and Cook Inlet include the black-legged kittiwake and the glaucous-winged gull, .This latter bird is also often referred to as the Homer sea gull. These Homer seagulls are omnivorous and highly opportunistic gulls that feed on almost anything available. The sooty shearwater skims over the waves in search of krill, fish, squid, and other foods in the outer Kachemak Bay. These birds breed in New Zealand and winter in Alaska. The pelagic cormorant does not have oil glands and hangs its wings out to dry. Northern fulmars nest in the Barren Islands, so the best way to see them is from the ferry or charter boats. The forked-tailed storm petrel also nests in the Barren Islands but can erratically be seen off the Homer Spit when it comes to feed on plankton. The red-faced cormorant is rarely found outside of Alaska. It is easy to see on Gull Island and is sought after by birders.

At the visitor center, I learned that the beaches of Pribilof Islands echo with the roar of close to one million northern fur seals as bulls fight for their territories and cows give birth to their pups. Visitors are also serenaded by the cries of more than three million seabirds nesting on the island's soaring cliffs. This extraordinary abundance of diversity has earned the Pribilof Islands the moniker of "Galapagos of the north."

The contours of the seafloor west of the Pribilofs hold the secret to the island's biological wealth. At the edge of the shallow continental shelf, Bering Sea plunges to a depth of 1,000 feet or more. Here, currents tumble and rise, mixing all sorts of nutrients that feed the food chain that supports the Pribilof's seabirds. Female fur seals run further afield. They chase small schools of pollock and squid 60 to 100 miles offshore. The seals can remain hunting at sea for 4–10 days. The Pribilof Islands are home to more than 80 percent of all red-legged kittiwakes as well as to tiny mammals called shrews. A shrew looks like a long-nosed mouse.

At the visitor center in Homer, otter and fox pelts were hung up on the wall to allow visitors to see what the hunters were killing. Thankfully, much has changed over time. For humanity, besides the cruelty seen with this practice, the Industrial Revolution produced new material used to insulate against the frigid weather. There was no reason or excuse to hunt these beautiful creatures to extinction. We now need to protect them from those who do not know any better.

We left the visitor center brimming with a treasure trove of history and knowledge—so rich and profound that it will take us a long time to fully digest and explore further. This center is truly one of the finest I have ever had the privilege to visit. My heartfelt congratulations go out to the visionaries who brought it to life and to the dedicated individuals who tirelessly devote their time and passion to educating the public within its inspiring halls. Their work is a gift to every visitor who walks through its doors.

BAYCREST OVERLOOK

After leaving the visitor center, we drove north along the Sterling Highway and stopped at Baycrest Overlook, one of Homer's most iconic viewpoints. From this vantage point, we enjoyed panoramic views of Kachemak Bay, the Kenai Mountains, and the Homer Spit. Informational signs detailed the local geography, wildlife, and history, while nearby gardens and fields of bright pink fireweed added to the scene's beauty.

For horticulturists and botanists, the overlook is a treasure trove. A mix of native trees, wildflowers, and cultivated ornamental plants thrive here, reflecting the rich biodiversity of the Kenai Peninsula.

The day was packed with discoveries, from learning about Alaska's maritime history to soaking in its natural beauty. As the day came to a close, I felt even more connected to this incredible place and its wonders. Here are the vegetations that can be found in this area.

Trees

Sitka spruce (*Picea sitchensis*)

- A dominant evergreen in coastal Alaska, Sitka spruce is characterized by sharp needles and dense branches, providing shelter for wildlife.

Black cottonwood (*Populus trichocarpa*)

- Known for its fast growth, this deciduous tree has large, glossy leaves and thrives in moist soils along riverbanks.

Alder (*Alnus spp.*)

- Species like red and Sitka alder are common, enriching the soil with nitrogen and thriving in wet environments.

Mountain hemlock (*Tsuga mertensiana*)

- Found in higher elevations or forest edges, this tree features soft needles and creates dense, shaded habitats.

Bushes and Shrubs

Devil's club (*Oplopanax horridus*)

- A spiny shrub that grows in shaded, moist areas. Despite its intimidating appearance, it plays a vital ecological role.

ELDERBERRY (*SAMBUCUS RACEMOSA*)

- Produces white flowers that mature into bright red berries, a food source for birds and wildlife. (Note: Cook before human consumption.)

WILD RASPBERRY (*RUBUS IDAEUS*)

- Thorny bushes with sweet red berries, found along trails and in open spaces.

SALMONBERRY (*RUBUS SPECTABILIS*)

- A shrub with bright orange or red berries and large toothed leaves, thriving in wet environments.

WILLOW (*SALIX* SPP.)

- Slender, flexible shrubs often found near water, with narrow leaves and branches.

WILDFLOWERS

FIREWEED (*CHAMAENERION ANGUSTIFOLIUM*)

- Iconic for its tall, pink-purple flower spikes, fireweed blooms in mid- to late summer and is a pioneer in disturbed soils.

LUPINE (*LUPINUS NOOTKATENSIS*)

- Produces stunning blue to purple flowers and is commonly seen in open meadows and along roadsides.

COW PARSNIP (*HERACLEUM MAXIMUM*)

- A towering plant with broad leaves and clusters of white flowers. Caution: Its sap can cause skin irritation.

DWARF DOGWOOD (*CORNUS CANADENSIS*)

- Also known as bunchberry, this ground cover features small white flowers and red berries, forming dense mats in shaded areas.

CHOCOLATE LILY (*FRITILLARIA CAMSCHATCENSIS*)

- A unique wildflower with brownish-purple, bell-shaped blooms found in moist meadows and woods.

YARROW (*ACHILLEA MILLEFOLIUM*)

- Hardy and versatile, yarrow displays clusters of small white or pink flowers and is a common sight along trails.

NOOTKA ROSE (*ROSA NUTKANA*)

- A fragrant wild rose with pink flowers and bright red rose hips, growing as a bushy shrub.

327

GRASSES AND GROUND COVER

BEACH PEA (*LATHYRUS JAPONICUS*)

- A low-growing, vine-like plant with purple flowers, typically found along beaches

SEDGES (*CAREX* SPP.)

- Grass-like plants with spiked flowers, thriving in wet meadows and along streams.

MOSSES AND LICHENS

- A variety of mosses and lichens cover rocks and forest floors, adding rich texture and color to the landscape.

SUMMARY

In summer, Baycrest Overlook transforms into a vibrant tapestry of lush Sitka spruce forests, fields of colorful wildflowers like fireweed and lupine, and thickets of salmonberry and elderberry bushes. These plants not only create a breathtaking natural display but also support a thriving ecosystem of birds, pollinators, and small mammals. The blend of towering trees, blooming flowers, and dense shrubs makes this iconic spot a must-visit for anyone exploring Homer and the Kenai Peninsula.

ORNAMENTAL FLOWERS AT BAYCREST OVERLOOK GARDENS IN HOMER, ALASKA

The city of Homer takes pride in maintaining vibrant gardens at Baycrest Overlook, showcasing a variety of ornamental flowers that thrive in Alaska's cooler, coastal climate. These gardens are carefully designed to provide colorful, fragrant, and hardy displays for visitors during the summer months. Below are some of the common ornamental flowers you'll find:

PANSIES (*VIOLA TRICOLOR VAR. HORTENSIS*)

- Known for their cheerful, multi-colored blooms, pansies thrive in cool temperatures. Their vibrant hues—ranging from purple and yellow to white—make them a favorite in Homer's gardens.

PETUNIAS (*PETUNIA SPP.*)

- These versatile flowers provide bright, trumpet-shaped blooms in colors like pink, purple, and red. Petunias are a staple in Baycrest's ornamental plantings due to their long flowering period and bold appearance.

MARIGOLDS (*TAGETES SPP.*)

- With their golden-yellow, orange, and red hues, marigolds

are not only visually striking but also naturally repel pests. They are frequently incorporated into Homer's gardens for their practical and aesthetic value.

ALYSSUM (*LOBULARIA MARITIMA*)

- This low-growing plant produces clusters of tiny, fragrant flowers in white or purple, making it ideal for borders or ground cover. Its delicate charm and pleasant scent are highlights in public garden designs.

SNAPDRAGONS (*ANTIRRHINUM MAJUS*)

- Snapdragons bring vertical interest to the gardens with their tall, spiked blooms. Available in a variety of colors, they add structure and elegance to the floral displays.

GERANIUMS (*PELARGONIUM SPP.*)

- Geraniums are a favorite for their durability and showy blossoms in pink, red, and white. These flowers are commonly planted in containers and garden beds, ensuring continuous color throughout the season.

DAHLIAS (*DAHLIA SPP.*)

- Famous for their large, dramatic blooms in shades of

pink, red, orange, and purple, dahlias are a showstopper in Homer's gardens. Their bushy growth adds depth and vibrancy to the displays.

CALENDULA (CALENDULA OFFICINALIS)

- These hardy flowers, with their sunny orange and yellow blooms, are perfect for Homer's climate. Besides their ornamental value, calendulas are also known for their medicinal properties.

BEGONIAS (BEGONIA SPP.)

- Begonias bring a splash of brilliance with their waxy leaves and bright flowers. Often used in hanging baskets and garden beds, they enhance the seasonal charm of Baycrest Overlook.

LAVENDER (LAVANDULA SPP.)

- Though not native to Alaska, lavender is occasionally featured for its aromatic purple flowers and soothing scent. Its inclusion adds a touch of elegance to the gardens.

SUMMARY

The carefully curated gardens at Baycrest Overlook feature a blend of hardy annuals and perennials, selected for their resilience in

Alaska's cool summers and their ability to provide stunning color and texture. From the cheerful pansies and marigolds to the fragrant lavender and striking dahlias, these flowers create a welcoming and picturesque environment. The gardens not only delight visitors with their beauty but also reflect Homer's commitment to celebrating nature's resilience and charm.

In addition, the below plants are a few more present in the garden.

These sites were so awesome, I kept thinking about how hard it would be to say goodbye at the end of this trip to Alaska, both its wilderness and its people. There aren't too many places in the world that I have felt so strongly about.

FIREWEED

CHINESE
GLOBEFLOWERER

GOOSEFOOT

POT MARIGOLD

BROAD-PETALED
GERANIUM

GARDEN COSMOS

AVENS

DANCING LADY ORCHID

WATER AVENS

EUROPEAN COLUMBINE

CANDLE LARKSPUR

Baycrest Overlook

CHAPTER 20

AUGUST 1

It was a beautiful day—the sun was shining, the sky was blue, and there was not much traffic heading down the Homer Spit. We drove down the Spit to get to the *Foxfire* by 7:30 a.m. Even though we had done this many times before, it was always a great and beautiful drive. It was a breathtaking and a desirous ritual; it felt like our very first time. As a matter of fact, it would not be bad to drive to the end of the Spit, turn around, and drive back and forth over and over again. It might sound obsessive, but it is just that magnificent. The essence of fulfillment is nearly indescribable, enveloping one in profound contentment. For sure, it is one of the most beautiful drives in the world, with the water of Kachemak Bay in front of the Kenai Mountains—a truly spectacular sight.

When we arrived at parking lot 3, we turned in to find a space. We paid $10 for the entire day, stepped out of the car, and put on our Grundéns gear over our layered clothes right there in the parking lot. With half our bodies inside the car and the other half outside, we managed to put on our woolen socks. Finally, the last piece of our attire was the BOGS boots we had purchased in Homer a few days earlier.

Taking a deep breath of fresh air, we made our way to the marina, heading down the aluminum ramp that led to the floating dock. The ramp was steep due to low tide—about a 45-degree angle—so I held onto its railings as we carefully walked down to avoid slipping. Once we reached the floating dock, we turned right and walked until we arrived at the *Foxfire*. We boarded the vessel for the trip, scheduled to depart at 7:30 a.m. and return by midday.

The *Foxfire* was about the same size as the *Spirit* but slightly smaller, with less seating capacity. Onboard, we were welcomed by Captain Grant and his two crew members, James and Luke. We received two colored zip ties, which we would use to tag the fish we caught. One color was for halibut 18 inches or shorter, and the other was for halibut of any size larger than 18 inches.

Many passengers would bring up smaller halibut, tagging the ones closest to 18 inches first, then waiting to catch their largest fish to use their second tag. Everyone usually waited to tag their biggest halibut before resting their rods. There was a limit of two fish per person, and anything caught beyond that had to be thrown back. There was no sense in harming a fish that couldn't be kept.

We continued fishing until the last passenger caught their limit, provided it wasn't past the hour we needed to start heading back to shore. Over the past few days, having fished on both the *Foxfire* and the *Spirit*, I realized the commitment these vessels made to their passengers. Even if just one passenger stubbornly held out to catch their largest halibut, as if holding the boat hostage, the crew would respectfully wait.

I would watch as that last person caught and released several fish, sometimes ten or more, before finally catching their biggest one. Meanwhile, 20 other passengers were waiting and hoping they'd catch it soon. I often wondered what difference it really made to bring in an 18-inch fish versus a 23-inch one. It wasn't about the fillet yield—the method of filleting could account for any difference. Perhaps it was more about ego and pride in the size of the catch.

Personally, I wouldn't have had the heart to keep so many people waiting. On a few occasions, I thought it was ridiculous. I always kept whatever fish I caught within my limit so we could head back sooner. Either way, by 12 p.m., the boat had to start heading back, no matter what.

Fishing in the Bay of Alaska was a lot of fun and a lot of work. We would usually lower the line to about 200 feet, baited with herring, sardine, or cod. If we caught cod, we often used it as bait to save money since herring was more expensive. By the end of the trip, after hauling up a 20-pound halibut with a five-pound weight from the ocean floor repeatedly, I would feel completely drained.

When passengers finished fishing, they often returned to the cabin to rest. A few of us remained outside on the stern for the ride home, soaking up the crisp, cool air. Standing at the stern, we could breathe fresh air and admire the waters and mountains instead of staring through glass windows from inside the cabin.

The ride back to the dock usually took about two hours, giving the crew enough time to fillet the fish, clean the boat, and allow passengers to take pictures with their catch. These photos became cherished memories and trophies to take home.

By the later days of our trip, Lauri and I didn't need more pictures. After landing at the dock, the Homer Spit Fish Processing Company would meet us. They cleaned and bagged the fish, and all we had to do was hand them over. The company would vacuum-pack and freeze them, ready for pickup or shipment home. Their service was excellent, and I would highly recommend them.

After nine days of fishing, we had a lot of fish stored. We were leaving with four boxes filled with halibut and cod to take to the airport. One of the nicest gestures Alaska Airlines offers is free transportation of fish caught in Alaska. It's a wonderful service, and I would gladly recommend flying with them. From the onset of our trip, Alaska Airlines impressed us. Our baggage from Newark made it through connections undisturbed, and we received it intact upon arrival in King Salmon two days later. Kudos to Alaska Airlines—I wouldn't hesitate to fly with them again.

Having caught our limit for the day, we returned to the Homer marina by 1 p.m. The next day, we would fly to Anchorage, leaving Homer in the morning. We planned to pick up our fillets from the Homer Processing Fish Company and bring them onboard for the flight to Anchorage. There, we would meet Nick from AK Trophy Expediters (also known as Alaska Anchorage Fish Storage and Shipping). He was holding our boxes of sockeye salmon. Nick would combine the salmon with the halibut and cod from Homer and ship all the boxes overnight to Newark. We would retrieve them the day after our arrival.

Tonight was our last night in Alaska. We had dinner at the house and packed for the trip back to the lower 48. It was a sad night for me. I fell in love with Alaska all over again and was deeply thankful to have returned. Alaska did right by me, and I can't wait to revisit and reacquaint myself with its many wonders.

Chapter 21

August 2

It was a very nice day—a bit chilly in the morning, but the sun was shining. After sipping some coffee, we headed down Highway 101 toward the Homer Spit. We worked hard to catch all that fish, not to mention that it also cost us a bundle.

We proceeded to the cash register, paid a handsome amount of money after fishing for nine days, and left with a lot of fillets of halibut, salmon and cod. We loaded the boxed fish into our SUV, which filled it to the brim. Turning out of the parking lot, we headed north to the airport, which was only 10 minutes away. Traffic was light as it was still early morning.

We drove through the airport's gate into the parking lot, unloaded our luggage and boxed fish, and brought it to the counter, where it was processed for the flight. As I looked at the tarmac, I could see only one airplane. It was a twin turboprop plane with the Alaska Ravn sign on it. There was another emblem on its side spelling "Nanooks." This other sign on the plane of Nanook was referring to the symbol that represents the polar bear in the Inuit language. If you happened to be an Inuit, you would know what the word meant. The Inuit, one of the original settlers of Alaska, saw the polar bear as being the most powerful and mighty, and felt that it was symbolic man. This is the reason Ravn airlines had it on its fuselage.

Checking into the airport in Homer. Going home with our catch. We will be eating delicious meals for quite a while. On the fuselage I see Nanook. This word represents the Polar Bear. The Polar Bear is a symbol of power & might.

The plane took off on time, seating approximately 20 passengers comfortably. The mountain ranges surrounding the airport, the Kenai, were so beautiful that they conjured passionate memories of my experience in Alaska. The mountainous peaks and plateaus appeared abundant with evergreen forests covering their sides. Some of the mountains were so tall that they penetrated the cotton-like clouds above them. The winds were mellow, and the flight was smooth, not bumpy.

The trip this evening would take us from Anchorage back to Newark, New Jersey

We arrived in Anchorage about 45 minutes later and walked off the plane to the baggage claim. As soon as we saw our four fish boxes on the conveyor belt, we called Nick from Anchorage Fish Storage and Shipping Service. He met us at the gate and took the boxes of fish back to his storage, where he would prepare them for shipment to Newark the next day.

A couple of hours later, we boarded a flight to Portland, Oregon, where we had a layover for a few hours. While in Portland,

I had the pleasure of going into a lounge for the first time in my life. The lounge served catered food and had comfortable chairs, recliners, and tables. It was part of Alaska Airlines, and what a great experience it turned out to be.

After spending a couple of hours there, we boarded our connecting flight to Newark, which took another eight hours. We landed at Newark around 7 a.m. the following Saturday morning.

CHAPTER 22

AUGUST 3

I was home now. I woke up in my comfortable bed and beautiful surroundings. Looking out my bedroom window, no, it wasn't the Kachemak Bay, but rather my beautiful Barnegat Bay. I was still feeling good, surrounded by water, even though separated by thousands of miles from Alaska.

I started thinking about the connection. What was it that I felt? I searched my mind and thought that 70 percent of our world is water. Water flows from everywhere to everywhere. Today, a drop in the ocean or bay from Alaska could have traveled into the waters of Barnegat Bay. Nobody knows, but it is certainly possible and even probable. The connection by water, which could have come from the Mediterranean, the Gulf of America, or the Pacific Ocean, can now also be here in Barnegat Bay.

The circle of life exists, even for a drop of water, anywhere in the world. Imagine if we had the ability to trace that drop; then we would know from where it had come.

As I opened my eyes, I could see our three dogs—Rosie, Ruby, and Tinsel. They looked happy. I think they might have missed me. If only they had known what a phenomenal experience I had in Alaska and how much I enjoyed its surroundings, they probably would have wanted to make the trip with me.

I could not wait to drive back to Newark Airport to pick up the salmon, halibut, and cod that we had caught in Alaska. Nick did a great job getting them there in a very reasonable time and at a reasonable cost. I drove to the airport the following day and picked them up. They were a lot of weight!

The experience will remain with us for the rest of our lives. We loved the fish, the wonders of the Alaskan landscape, its historical culture, and its people. We know that soon, it will not be enough. When we feel the Alaskan itch, we will have to return.

Acknowledgments

Having people support your passion is indeed a blessing. I would not have been able to write this book without the help of some extraordinary people who supported my passion, desire, and vision. It would have been an empty dream without their guidance and assistance. They have listened to me, encouraged me, and allowed me to pursue my dreams.

First, I must give an enormous thanks to my friend Lauri, who traveled with me from New Jersey to Alaska and guided me through airports, buses, and cars. She not only helped me find my way around strange places, but she also helped me transport my many suitcases and bags. Lauri made all the arrangements for transportation. We had to take flights within days of each other to two separate areas in southeastern Alaska, which meant we had to make some extra stops, stay over in Anchorage, and shuttle between a couple of planes.

Lauri is very competent, skilled, and valuable and a loving friend. She truly cares. She has always been there as my extra set of eyes. There is nothing that she does without true dedication and enthusiasm, and she always stays completely focused. I have seen her undeterred, performing a task for many hours at a time without even getting out of a chair, working nonstop on a job until it was done well.

With her keen perception and judgment, she has helped me face some very challenging moments. As embarrassing as it may be, let it be known that she also caught most of the fish we brought home. In addition, she is a gifted chef who was greatly admired and appreciated at the lodge by everyone. Robert the chef especially had a special fondness for her, as the two spent much time discussing recipes for the evening meals. Robert even told me that she gave him a lot of creative ideas and inspiration.

Between Lauri's ideas and Robert's tools and hands, we all ate very well at the lodge. Dinners included 15 people most nights. At our stay at the Airbnb in Homer, Alaska, Lauri was the only chef there and I was always delighted with her skills. I have many pictures of her dishes that she prepared for us. Lauri, you prepared some excellent meals! Thank you very much for everything you have done and especially for helping me out. There is no lazy bone in your body. Thank you very much!

A very big thanks to my children—Victoria, David, Julianne,

Jonathan, and Jennifer—for allowing me to take the time to follow my passions and for forgiving me for not spending as much time as I would have liked to with each of you. You have filled my life in more ways than you will ever know. I know that you are busy with your colleges, nursing school, and work, but you are doing everything that young adults need to do. Please follow your dreams and passions, just as you have allowed me to follow mine. Thank you for that opportunity, and I am eternally grateful for your support, smiles, laughter, and love.

My next and even bigger thanks is to all those people who made my dream and our trip come true and very meaningful. Your daily hard work did not go unnoticed. I saw how dedicated you were to your work and guests.

I am first dedicating many thanks to the people at the Alagnak Lodge in Alaska. Tony Behm, the owner of the Alagnak Lodge, has kept it running very well and making his guests feel right at home with his warm and charming personality. Tony, you are superbly exceptional! I know that you are strong, loving, extremely committed, very hard-working, and bright. Your crew love and respect you. They also said the most wonderful words about you.

Because the Alagnak Lodge is off the grid, Tony and his staff make every effort to commit to close and interdependent relationships. The lodge depends on their sustenance. They have constructed, developed, created, and maintained their own water systems, sewer systems, communication equipment, two giant generators to supply the lodge with electricity, and even a spare one in case the one running breaks down. In addition, they have about a dozen boats with marine outboard engines that require attention that they have kept running well. Tony has not only been working hard for the many years that he has owned it, but he has dedicated his life to it. And that shows when one is there as a guest or an employee.

Sometimes Tony has returned to the lodge the next season to find that it had been ransacked by locals and in need of rebuilding and resupplying. Tony also serves as the spiritual leader for the lodge. Even though he lives in Hawaii, he has spent many years traveling to the Alagnak for the summer, starting in late May or early June, at the cost of leaving his family behind in Hawaii. Besides this great personal sacrifice, I believe he also follows his passion. Thank you so much to you again, Tony, for doing all that you have done in sharing your passions with us. Without you, this lodge would either not have existed or not have been as meaningful.

Being the spiritual leader of the lodge, Tony reinforces everybody's spirits when things do not go exactly as planned. It is not easy to live off the grid in Alaska, even in the summer. Things happen and break down. There are also so many different personalities to deal with, and at times things do not go as planned. Tony has been there to put it all together and bring the positive vibes and raise spirits whenever needed. He sees a glass as being half full, not half empty. Tony is the greatest. Without him or his presence, how could I have fulfilled my dream and supported my passion? We all owe you big-time. A big thanks to you.

The other big thanks goes to the staff at the lodge. Gavin, our guide, is a very responsible young man. In his early 20s, he has spent the past three summers at the lodge. Not only is he responsible but also wise for his age. He took us out every day to fish, observe nature, and discover the Alagnak River. He always went out of his way to show us how important our being happy meant to him.

Robert the chef, who later in the story gets into trouble, made the best food and desserts. Robert, we say thank you for the great meals that you prepared and for your friendship. We are sorry you got yourself into some trouble, but hopefully you will work that out. Robert, you are absolutely charismatic. There are not many people whom we meet who are as charming as you are, who have your warmth along with the ability to let their hair hang down. Robert made us feel special, especially when he liked you—and not so special when he did not. He appeared explorative and spontaneous, a free spirit of sorts. He lived life in search of new experiences, traveling or exploring without long-term commitments. Impulsive, to say the least.

Robert had a knack for following his instincts, embracing spontaneity and the excitement of the unknown. He thrived on challenges and was fearless in the face of uncertainty, approaching life as an adventure to uncover new discoveries—whether physical, emotional, or intellectual. A curious and open-hearted individual, Robert brought warmth and enthusiasm to every situation. His culinary skills left a lasting impression on us, and we're grateful for the incredible meals he shared. As Robert continues his journey, we wish him all the best and know his bold spirit will lead him to great places.

Peter, a 35-year-old mechanic of Irish descent, is Mat's brother, who also worked as a guide at the lodge. Known as the group's leader and Tony's trusted right-hand man, Peter combined confidence, ambition, and a tireless drive to expand his practical knowledge. His goal-oriented mindset and unwavering determination inspired those around him, as he consistently achieved the targets he set with precision and focus. Passionate about his craft and committed to excellence, Peter's dedication to doing his best in everything he undertook was admirable. His pursuit of success was a reflection of his hardworking nature, and his leadership left a positive mark on the team.

There was nothing that Peter could not do, or so it seemed. If he had a task that was unfamiliar to him, he would find out the information needed, face the challenge, and usually succeed. He was very responsible when it came to repairing and maintaining anything that was powered at the lodge. This included the generators that ran all the electric at our site, the outboard engines on the John boats, and the water pump that inhaled the water from the Alagnak River and pumped it over the riverbank, which was steep, and into the filtering area, where it was purified of wastes from the river.

His brother Mat, slightly younger than Peter, has a very nice temperament and disposition. A calming sort of personality, a lot more laid-back than Peter. Probably a bit less driven, and if I had to guess, a bit less ambitious. I had a feeling that he was more of a spiritual seeker than Peter, not so much a workaholic or a perfectionist. His sense of spirituality was highlighted by the presence of his dog Dark Star. The dog wasn't just a companion; Dark Star was a spiritual bridge connecting the two divinely. Mat was also a guide at the lodge.

Dark Star would come around every day to greet everyone, as if to say good morning to all. When he made the rounds, between the guides on the dock, someone would throw Dark Star a fallen, large branch of a tree, and Dark Star would immediately dive into the icy water of the Alagnak and give it chase. It was amazing to see this black, humongous dog dive into the river, especially when the current was running. Because when the current was running on the Alagnak between tides, it would be very strong. As big and as tall as Dark Star was, I had never seen this amazing dog bark. When I spoke with Mat about my curiosity oabout the non-barking dog of his, Mat replied in his usual quiet and serene voice, "You should see him bark when he is chasing a bear up a tree."

Then there was Wade, who was both young (early 20s) and young at heart. Lauri and I were at the lodge with only two other guests at the time. It had become known to us that most of the other guests would be arriving the following week. We were thus the only customers at this lodge for the time. Each pair of people required one guide. Having very few guests, which was unusual at this time, left some of the other guides free to enjoy more of their day. Wade, having little to do, sat in the dining room, often on his phone—until he heard and saw Robert charging Mat with the intent of hurting him, at which point Wade jumped out of his chair like a lit firecracker and came to Mat's rescue. Wade pinned Robert to the ground, and he and Mat held him down until others came to their aid. It just so happened that after this whole incident occurred, I learned that Wade, who was six-foot-two and 350 pounds, used to play football in high school. Thank you, Wade, for being responsive when needed, and I really understand that the cell phone is a useful part of life to prevent boredom and keep in touch with friends.

Everybody had huge respect for Glen. By appearance, he appeared to be the oldest and the most experienced guide at the lodge. He seemed to be a bit more analytical in his strategy. More of a master planner—always thinking about several steps ahead, making choices that aligned with his long-term plan to show his clients a good time and catch fish. I felt a sense of pragmatism in his approach to the day to come, always looking for the most efficient path to achieve his goals. He was soft-spoken like Mat, and when he was not on the Alagnak, he was down in Florida guiding Floridian anglers.

We spent the first leg of our trip, July 13–23, 2024, at the Alagnak Lodge at the edge of the Alagnak River. The second part of our trip, from July 24 to August 3, was spent in Homer, Alaska, more specifically the Homer Spit. I would like to thank the many people who helped us during our time in both areas. God bless you all. You were marvelous, passionate, kind, and very appreciated in all the efforts that you took to ensure our satisfaction.

A special thanks to Kathy, who works with Rainbow Tours at the Homer Spit. Kathy is a very dedicated employee for the Rainbow Tour Company. She has the ability to make people feel special, as if they are her only customer. Thank you, Kathy, for being there for us and making the arrangements for so many daily fishing trips. Continue keeping a tight shift because we know how busy things get. We will miss you too.

I would also like to extend our thanks to those involved with the visitor center in Homer. This great edifice looks like a battalion, an imposing brown brick stoned building. Once entered, it displays an elaborate treatise on the history of the region's people of southeast Alaska. It especially concentrates on the area of the Kachemak Bay and the Bay of Alaska, but it also extends beyond that. It deals with the story of the Inuit people and the history of the area and Alaska—all that has occurred in the past few hundred years. Their story and the story of how this area has come to be and developed is incredibly interesting. Keep up the great work you are all doing over there at the visitor center, and thank you so much.

We were sightseeing, shopping, discovering nature, and fishing at the Homer Spit for approximately 11 days. Each time that we drove through the Kachemak Bay we would end up in the Gulf of Alaska. We would like to thank all the captains and their mates for taking such good care of us and making our trip very enjoyable. To all of you, from all of us, thank you again. In particular, I would like to get specific about each boat and crew that we used.

I owe a big thanks to Captain Drew, who owns and runs the *Patriot*, and his mate Sam. Captain Drew is a very focused individual, and while speaking with him I discovered that he is also a responsible husband and father. Goal-oriented, he started his career in his late teens as a deckhand and eventually earned his captain's license. He worked hard and saved enough money to buy a beautiful 30-foot aluminum boat, which we experienced. I think he is a perfectionist and probably calculates every step before making a move, afraid of taking big chances. I have a feeling that he is security-focused, aiming for a steady job, a safe home, and a predictable environment, prioritizing safety above adventure, maybe even to a point of overthinking before acting. At least that was my impression. I thank Captain Drew for taking us fishing, showing us a good time, and bringing us home safely. In this boat, which was a whole-day trip, we went out significantly farther than on the other two larger boats that we booked for half-day fishing trips. I also want to thank Sam for working very hard, filleting the fish, and cleaning the boat nonstop on our trip. His efforts did not go unnoticed. You did a great job, Sam. Thank you.

In the morning, we went fishing on a boat called the *Firefox*, which was a half-day halibut fishing trip. The *Firefox* was a 60-foot monohull fishing boat. On board, we were welcomed by Captain Grant and his two crew members, James and Luke. Captain Grant, a middle-aged man, had long curly hair that rest at the lower end of his neck. Captain James seemed a bit laid-back but very content—a fellow who, for the most part, would go with the flow. Carefree, he enjoyed the present moment without worrying too much about the future or long-term plans, seemingly believing that things would work out for the best, even without a detailed plan. He seemed to be a minimalist who focused on living a simple life without unnecessary stress or material goals, often choosing happiness over success.

Deckhand James was more explorative and spontaneous. I felt that James was a free spirit who lived life in search of new experiences, traveling or exploring without long-term commitments. On the other hand, he did own a restaurant in Homer that served dinners.

So I felt that even though he was a free spirit, there was another side to him that was driven, ambitious, and goal-oriented. He was very helpful and attentive in baiting our hooks and helped us to bring the fish on board. He was outgoing and extroverted and we liked him. Thank you, James, for taking such good care of us.

Crew member Luke was very young, perhaps even a teenager. He seemed a bit uncertain and aimless. Because of his age, he may have been drifting and moving through life without clear goals, perhaps reacting more to circumstances than creating his own path, probably because of lack of experience at this point in his life. Thank you, Luke, for helping us out.

In the afternoons, we were scheduled on another boat, the *Spirit*, a 65-foot vessel that would leave in the early afternoon and come back in the evening. During each of these days we fished with Captain James and his crew, Patrick and Bryce. Captain James was very quiet and we didn't see much of him, maybe because Patrick and Bryce were able to hold their own. I really never got a chance to speak with Captain James on the *Spirit*. At the same time, we were very busy catching fish and had a lot of interactions with Captain James's crew.

Patrick was a tall and slender man, with long hair tied into a ponytail that was curled onto the top of his head. His face had a chiseled look. You could see the length of his hair at the end of each trip when he would untie it and let it down. He did have some beautiful dirty blond hair with a natural wave. Had he let it loose during the fishing trip, his hair would have been a distraction on the job. Patrick's personality, if I had to guess, was rebellious and nonconforming. He was probably actively resisting societal expectations, forging his own path in defiance of the norm. Probably a rule-breaker, preferring to challenge the status quo and embrace unconventional choices. This is my guess, and of course I can be off track.

Bryce, on the other hand, was quieter, soft-spoken, but very quick in his maneuvers, pacing, cleaning, filleting halibut, and helping everybody on board. He kept more to himself, seeming always busy with work and keeping these conversations short. Bryce appeared somewhat less self-assured and was probably the kind of guy who put people's needs above himself. That was my general impression. Both he and Patrick were very nice, professional, helpful, and accommodating. Thank you both so much for making us feel at home and welcomed every day on your boat.

REFERENCES

HOMER, ALASKA - GENERAL INFORMATION

1. **"A History of Homer, Alaska"** - Focuses on the town's origins and development.

2. **"Homer: The Halibut Fishing Capital of the World"** - Insight into the town's identity and tourism.

3. **Homer Chamber of Commerce and Visitor Center** - Source of travel guides and local tips.

4. **Kachemak Bay Research Reserve** - Research articles and papers.

5. **"Living in Homer, Alaska: A Small Town Guide"** - Personal experiences of residents.

FISHING IN HOMER, ALASKA

6. **"Fishing in Homer: A Comprehensive Guide"** - Techniques and spots for anglers.

7. **Alaska Department of Fish and Game (ADF&G) Fishing Regulations** - For those interested in fishing legally.

8. **"The Best Fishing Charters in Homer, Alaska"** - Lists of charter companies and what to expect.

9. **"Homer Halibut Fishing: Tips from Local Experts"** - Guide to catching halibut.

10. **"Tales from Homer's Fishing Docks"** - Stories from commercial fishers.

11. **Kenai Peninsula Fishing Reports** - Weekly updates on fish movement.

Marine Life and Ecosystems

12. **"The Marine Life of Kachemak Bay"** - Overview of marine species.

13. **"Alaska's Salmon Species"** - Detailed study of different salmon in Alaska waters.

14. **"Understanding the Tides in Cook Inlet"** - How tides influence fish behavior.

15. **"Crabbing and Shrimping in Homer"** - Overview of crabbing and shrimping opportunities.

16. **Kachemak Bay Critical Habitat Area** - Conservation efforts in the bay.

Flora of Alaska

17. **"Wildflowers of Alaska"** - Guide to identifying Alaskan wildflowers.

18. **"Alaska's Native Plant Species"** - Resource for native vegetation.

19. **"Ornamental Gardens in Homer, Alaska"** - Gardens at Baycrest Overlook and beyond.

20. **"Mushrooms and Fungi of Alaska"** - Study of fungi in Alaska's temperate rainforest.

21. **Alaska Botanical Garden Resources** - Plant species and research.

22. **"Foraging in Alaska: Edible and Medicinal Plants"** - Foraging wild plants and their uses.

23. **"Conservation of the Alaskan Boreal Forest"** - Flora and plant ecosystem study.

24. **"Rare and Endangered Plants of Alaska"** - Conservation status and descriptions.

Sightseeing Tours and Nature Exploration

25. **"Top 10 Wildlife Viewing Tours in Homer"** - Reviews of local wildlife tours.

26. **"Birdwatching in Homer, Alaska"** - Guide to bird species and hotspots.

27. **"Homer Spit: A Traveler's Guide"** - Exploring Homer Spit and its activities.

28. **Alaska State Parks: Homer Section** - Trails and scenic spots in local parks.

29. **"Best Glacier Tours from Homer"** - Day trips to view glaciers.

30. **"Whale Watching Tours in Homer"** - Best seasons and companies.

31. **"Hiking Trails Around Homer"** - Trail guides for outdoor adventurers.

32. **"Photography Tours in Homer, Alaska"** - Guided tours for photography enthusiasts.

33. **Alaska Maritime National Wildlife Refuge** - Guides to the refuge and its tours.

34. **"Boat Tours in Kachemak Bay"** - Overview of boating tours.

35. **"Kayaking in Kachemak Bay"** - Water routes and rental companies.

Wildlife in Alaska

36. **"The Wildlife of Kachemak Bay"** - Fauna in the coastal ecosystem.

37. **"Alaska's Marine Mammals"** - Research on whales, otters, and seals.

38. **"Bald Eagles in Homer, Alaska"** - Study on the local bald eagle population.

39. **"Alaska Bear Viewing Tours"** - Where to spot grizzly and black bears.

40. **"Seabirds of Alaska"** - Comprehensive guide on the seabird species of Homer.

Local Culture and Events

41. **"Homer's Annual Shorebird Festival"** - Popular birdwatching festival.

42. **"The Arts Scene in Homer, Alaska"** - Overview of the art galleries and cultural events.

43. **"Fishing Tournaments in Homer"** - Local competition events.

44. **"Homer Farmers' Market Guide"** - Local produce and artisanal goods.

45. **"Dining in Homer, Alaska: Seafood and Local Cuisine"** - Best restaurants for fresh seafood.

46. **"Homesteading in Homer"** - History and practice of homesteading in the area.

Ecosystem and Environmental Studies

47. **"Impact of Climate Change on Alaska's Fisheries"** - Effects of warming on local fish.

48. **"Alaska's Sustainable Fishing Practices"** - Focus on fishing conservation.

49. **"Biodiversity of Alaska's Coastal Ecosystems"** - Research articles on marine and plant life.

50. **"Preserving Kachemak Bay's Marine Ecosystem"** - Studies on the bay's ecological health.

Cultural and Historical Exploration

51. **"Homer's Russian Heritage"** – The influence of Russian settlers on the town.

52. **"The Kachemak Bay Communities: Past and Present"** – Historical accounts of the indigenous peoples and early settlers.

53. **"The Historic Pratt Museum"** – Cultural exhibits and local history.

54. **"The Alaska Native Heritage Center"** – Focus on Native Alaskan culture.

55. **"Alaska Homesteaders: Living Off the Land"** – Personal stories of Alaskan pioneers.

56. **"Homer Public Library: Alaska History Resources"** – Collection of historical documents and accounts.

57. **"Pioneer and Maritime History of Alaska"** – Overview of the exploration of Alaskan waters.

Marine Research and Fisheries Studies

58. **"The Role of Halibut in Homer's Economy"** – Study on the importance of fishing to local livelihood.

59. **"Alaska's Commercial Fishing Industry"** – Overview of fish species caught commercially.

60. **"Sustainable Fisheries in Kachemak Bay"** – Sustainable fishing practices in Alaska.

61. **"Salmon Spawning in Cook Inlet"** – Research on salmon breeding patterns.

62. **"Deep-Sea Fishing in Alaska"** – Studies on fishing in deeper waters beyond the bay.

63. **"Bycatch Issues in Alaska's Commercial Fisheries"** – Concerns about unwanted marine life caught in nets.

64. **"Fisheries Management in Alaska"** – Overview of laws and regulations governing fishing practices.

65. **"The Impact of Overfishing on Alaska's Ecosystem"** – Research on how overfishing affects marine biodiversity.

Alaskan Flora and Wildlife Conservation

66. **"The Boreal Forests of Alaska"** – Plant species and forest ecology in northern Alaska.

67. **"Plant Adaptations in the Arctic Tundra"** – How Alaskan plants survive in cold climates.

68. **"The Role of Pollinators in Alaska's Ecosystems"** – The interaction between native plants and pollinators.

Oceanography and Marine Ecosystem Studies

Tour Guides and Visitor Information

82. **"Helicopter Glacier Tours from Homer"** – Air-based tours of Alaska's famous glaciers.

83. **"Eco-Tourism in Homer"** – The rise of environmentally friendly travel options in the area.

84. **"Alaska's National Parks: A Visitor's Guide"** – Highlights of national parks within reach of Homer.

85. **"Day Cruises from Homer"** – Overview of boat tours around Kachemak Bay.

86. **"Aurora Borealis Viewing Tours in Alaska"** – Tips and guides for viewing the Northern Lights.

87. **"Scenic Drives Around Homer"** – Driving routes showcasing Alaska's natural beauty.

Marine Wildlife and Birdwatching Resources

88. **"Whales of Alaska: Identification and Migration"** – Study of whale species migrating through Homer.

89. **"Seabird Colonies in Kachemak Bay"** – Research on the nesting and feeding habits of seabirds.

90. **"Bird Migration Patterns Over Alaska"** – Studies on birds traveling through Alaska.

91. **"Orca and Humpback Whales in Cook Inlet"** – Research on local whale populations.

92. **"Alaska's Coastal Birdwatching Guide"** – Resources for spotting coastal bird species.

93. **"The Steller Sea Lion: Icon of Alaska's Waters"** – Studies on sea lion populations in the region.

94. **"Ecosystem Impact of Bald Eagles in Homer"** – The role of bald eagles in local ecosystems.

95. **"The Migration of Shorebirds to Kachemak Bay"** – Annual patterns of migrating shorebirds.

96. **"The Kittiwake: Alaska's Coastal Seabird"** – Research on the nesting habits of kittiwakes.

Ecology and Conservation Studies

97. **"Marine Protected Areas in Alaska"** – Efforts to protect sensitive marine environments.

98. **"Restoration of Salmon Streams in Alaska"** – Projects aimed at restoring salmon habitats.

99. **"Preserving the Wildlife of Alaska's National Wildlife Refuges"** – Overview of refuge efforts around Homer.

100. **"Reducing Human Impact on Kachemak Bay"** – Studies on conservation and human interaction.

101. **"The Impact of Tourism on Homer's Ecosystems"** – Balancing tourism and preservation.

102. **"Alaska's Marine Biodiversity Hotspots"** – Key areas with the highest biodiversity.

103. **"Plastic Pollution in Alaska's Coastal Waters"** – Research on marine pollution in remote areas.

Festivals and Events in Homer

104. **"Homer's Halibut Festival"** – A festival celebrating the local fishing industry.

105. **"Homer's Summer Concert Series"** – Local music events and outdoor performances.

106. **"The Alaska State Fair: Homer's Representation"** – Local booths and activities representing Homer at the state fair.

107. **"Homer Shorebird Festival: A Birder's Paradise"** – Annual event celebrating bird migration.

108. **"Kachemak Bay Science Conference"** – Gathering of scientists and researchers to discuss marine science.

109. **"Homer's Annual Film Festival"** – Showcasing films that highlight Alaska's wilderness and wildlife.

Fishing Regulations and Sustainable Practices

110. **"Alaska Fishing Regulations for 2024"** – Current fishing rules and limits.

111. **"How to Obtain a Fishing License in Alaska"** – Steps and requirements for fishing legally.

112. **"Catch and Release Practices in Homer"** – Ethical fishing methods to preserve species.

113. **"Sustainable Fishing Tours in Homer"** – Tour operators practicing sustainable methods.

114. **"Commercial Fishing Quotas in Alaska"** – Regulations on allowable catch for commercial fishers.

115. **"Managing Bycatch in Alaska's Fisheries"** – Solutions for minimizing non-target species capture.

116. **"Marine Protected Areas and Their Impact on Fishing"** – How no-fishing zones affect local fisheries.

117. **"The Importance of Hatcheries for Salmon Restoration"** – Role of hatcheries in maintaining salmon populations.

Alaska's National Parks and Nature Reserves

118. **"Exploring Kenai Fjords National Park"** – A guide to the nearby national park.

119. **"Katmai National Park: Brown Bear Viewing"** – Tips on visiting and viewing bears.

120. **"Hiking in Denali National Park"** – A guide to trails and wildlife viewing.

121. **"Wrangell-St. Elias National Park: The Largest in the U.S."** – Guide to Alaska's largest national park.

122. **"Chugach National Forest: A Natural Gem"** – Overview of outdoor activities near Homer.

Marine Research and Oceanography

123. **"The Role of Kelp Forests in Alaska's Marine Ecosystems"** – Study on the importance of kelp forests in supporting marine life.

124. **"Ocean Currents in the Gulf of Alaska"** – Research on how ocean currents affect local fisheries and marine biodiversity.

125. **"The Effect of Algal Blooms on Alaska's Marine Life"** – Understanding harmful algal blooms in Alaskan waters.

126. **"Coastal Erosion and Its Impact on Alaska's Fishing Communities"** – Studies on how erosion affects coastal towns like Homer.

127. **"Trophic Levels in Alaska's Marine Food Web"** – Exploration of predator-prey relationships in the marine environment.

128. **"The Impact of Melting Sea Ice on Alaska's Marine Species"** – How climate change is affecting the habitats of ice-dependent species.

129. **"Glacial Melt and Its Effects on the Marine Ecosystem"** – The influence of glacial melt on water temperatures and marine biodiversity.

130. **"The Role of Zooplankton in the Alaskan Marine Food Chain"** – Research on zooplankton as a key food source for fish and marine mammals.

131. **"The Importance of Estuaries in Kachemak Bay"** – Studies on the critical habitats provided by estuarine environments.

132. **"Marine Snow and Its Role in Deep-Sea Ecosystems"** – Research on how marine snow supports deep-sea life in Alaska.

Climate Change and Environmental Impact

133. **"The Impact of Rising Ocean Temperatures on Alaska's Fisheries"** – Studies on how warming oceans affect fish populations.

134. **"Climate Change and Its Effects on Alaska's Tundra Ecosystems"** – Research on the impact of changing temperatures on tundra plant and animal life.

135. **"Permafrost Thawing and Its Environmental Consequences in Alaska"** – Effects of thawing permafrost on ecosystems and human infrastructure.

136. **"The Role of Carbon Sequestration in Alaska's Forests"** – Studies on how Alaska's forests absorb carbon and mitigate climate change.

137. **"Sea Level Rise and Its Impact on Alaska's Coastal Communities"** – Research on how rising sea levels are affecting towns like Homer.

138. **"The Effects of Ocean Acidification on Alaska's Shellfish"** – Study on how acidifying oceans are impacting shellfish populations.

139. **"Shifts in Wildlife Migration Patterns Due to Climate Change"** – Studies on how climate change is altering the migration of birds and marine mammals.

140. **"Adaptation Strategies for Alaska's Fishing Industry Amid Climate Change"** – Research on how the fishing industry is adapting to environmental changes.

Local Arts and Culture

141. **"Homer's Art Scene: Local Artists and Galleries"** – Overview of the artistic community in Homer and its influence on the local culture.

142. **"Traditional Alaskan Native Art and Crafts"** – Exploration of indigenous art forms and their cultural significance.

143. **"The Role of the Bunnell Street Arts Center in Homer's Cultural Life"** – Study on the impact of this local arts center.

144. **"Music and Festivals in Homer: Celebrating Alaska's Heritage"** – Overview of music festivals and their connection to local culture.

145. **"Indigenous Alaskan Storytelling Traditions"** – Exploration of traditional oral storytelling in Alaska's native communities.

146. **"Crafting with Driftwood: Art from the Shores of Homer"** – A look at how local artists use natural materials in their work.

147. **"Sustainable Tourism and the Arts in Homer"** – Study on how tourism supports and affects the arts community.

148. **"The Influence of Alaska's Wilderness on Local Artists"** – Analysis of how the natural environment inspires local art and photography.

149. **"The Homer Bookstore: Alaska's Literary Hub"** – Overview of the importance of local bookstores in Alaska's literary scene.

Fisheries Science and Aquaculture

150. **"The Role of Fish Hatcheries in Alaska's Salmon Recovery"** – Research on the impact of hatcheries on salmon populations.

151. **"Aquaculture in Alaska: Opportunities and Challenges"** – Study on the growing aquaculture industry and its potential.

152. **"Sustainable Fishing Practices in Homer"** – Overview of how local fishers are practicing sustainability.

153. **"Fishery-Induced Evolution: Impacts on Alaskan Fish Species"** – Research on how fishing pressures are affecting the evolution of fish populations.

154. **"Ocean Ranching of Salmon in Alaska"** – Study on the practice of ocean ranching and its effects on wild fish populations.

155. **"Impact of Commercial Fishing on Marine Biodiversity in Alaska"** – Research on the consequences of large-scale fishing on marine ecosystems.

156. **"Alaska's Role in Global Seafood Markets"** – Study on how Alaska's fisheries contribute to global seafood trade.

157. **"Fishing Gear Innovations to Reduce Bycatch"** – Exploration of technological advancements aimed at reducing the capture of non-target species.

158. **"Habitat Restoration Efforts for Alaska's Anadromous Fish"** – Study on efforts to restore habitats for species like salmon that migrate between freshwater and saltwater.

159. **"Alaska's Shellfish Industry: Opportunities for Growth"** – Research on the potential for expanding shellfish farming in the state.

Outdoor Recreation and Adventure Tourism

160. **"Backpacking Trails Near Homer"** – Guide to long-distance hiking and camping opportunities.

161. **"Homer's Best Camping Spots"** – Overview of camping locations near Kachemak Bay.

162. **"Kayaking Adventures in Kachemak Bay"** – Guide to kayaking routes and the wildlife you may encounter.

163. **"Winter Sports in Homer: Skiing and Snowshoeing"** – Overview of winter recreational opportunities around Homer.

164. **"Scuba Diving in Alaska's Cold Waters"** – An exploration of scuba diving spots and what to expect in Alaska's frigid waters.

165. **"Mountain Biking Trails Near Homer"** – Guide to mountain biking routes in the area.

166. **"Rock Climbing in Alaska: A Guide to Homer's Best Spots"** – Overview of climbing locations around Homer.

167. **"Overnight Wildlife Tours from Homer"** – Companies offering overnight stays and wildlife viewing in remote areas.

168. **"Sailing Adventures Around Kachemak Bay"** – Guide to sailboat charters and tours in the bay.

169. **"Exploring the Harding Icefield by Snowmobile"** – Overview of snowmobiling adventures around Homer and beyond.

Environmental Education and Community Initiatives

170. **"Environmental Education Programs at Kachemak Bay"** – Overview of local education efforts aimed at teaching sustainability.

171. **"The Role of the Center for Alaskan Coastal Studies in Environmental Education"** – Study on the impact of this educational institution.

172. **"Citizen Science in Homer: How Residents Help Protect the Environment"** – Study on how the local community engages in citizen science efforts.

173. **"Sustainable Living in Homer: A Guide to Off-the-Grid Living"** – Overview of how some residents are adopting off-grid lifestyles in Homer.

174. **"The Kachemak Heritage Land Trust: Preserving Alaska's Wild Lands"** – Study on local land preservation efforts.

175. **"Alaska's Marine Debris Cleanup Initiatives"** – Research on local efforts to reduce marine debris and plastic pollution.

176. **"Local Agriculture in Homer: Farming in the Far North"** – Study on how local farms operate in Homer's unique climate.

177. **"Organic Farming and Sustainable Practices in Alaska"** – Guide to local farms using organic and sustainable methods.

178. **"Youth Conservation Programs in Alaska"** – Overview of programs aimed at getting youth involved in environmental conservation.

179. **"Local Efforts to Combat Invasive Species in Kachemak Bay"** – Research on how local communities are addressing the problem of invasive species.

ALASKA'S INDIGENOUS COMMUNITIES AND CULTURAL PRESERVATION

180. **"Alaska Native Language Preservation"** – Efforts to revitalize and preserve indigenous languages.

181. **"Traditional Subsistence Fishing and Hunting Practices"** – Overview of indigenous fishing and hunting techniques and their cultural significance.

182. **"Indigenous Perspectives on Climate Change in Alaska"** – How Alaska's native communities are being affected by and responding to climate change.

183. **"The Role of Storytelling in Alaskan Native Cultures"** – Study on the importance of oral traditions in native communities.

184. **"The Alaska Federation of Natives: A History"** – Overview of the federation and its role in representing indigenous communities.

185. **"The Role of Potlatch Ceremonies in Alaskan Native Culture"** – Exploration of traditional potlatch gatherings and their significance.

186. **"Indigenous Knowledge in Environmental Stewardship"** – Study on how traditional knowledge is integrated into conservation efforts.

Alagnak River - General Information and Geography

1. **"Exploring the Alagnak Wild River: A Complete Guide"** – Overview of the river's history, geography, and significance.

2. **"Alagnak River National Wild and Scenic River System"** – U.S. National Park Service resources on the river.

3. **"The Alagnak River Basin: A Geological Study"** – Research on the river's geological formation and features.

4. **"Wild and Scenic: The Alagnak River in Southwest Alaska"** – Exploration of what makes the river unique.

5. **"Alaska's Alagnak River: A Remote Wilderness"** – A guide to the remote nature of the river and its surroundings.

6. **"Hydrology of the Alagnak River"** – Scientific study on the river's water flow and hydrological cycle.

7. **"The Role of the Alagnak River in the Bristol Bay Watershed"** – How the river contributes to the greater watershed of the region.

Fishing on the Alagnak River

8. **"Fly Fishing the Alagnak River: A Comprehensive Guide"** – Techniques and spots for fly fishing on the river.

9. **"Fishing for Trophy Rainbow Trout on the Alagnak River"** – Guide to fishing for rainbow trout on the river.

10. **"Alaska's King Salmon: Alagnak River Fishing"** – A detailed guide on catching king salmon in the river.

11. **"Salmon Runs on the Alagnak River"** – An overview of the timing and species involved in the salmon migrations.

12. **"Fly-Fishing Lodges on the Alagnak River"** – Directory of fishing lodges along the river for anglers.

13. **"The Best Fishing Charters on the Alagnak River"** – A guide to professional fishing tours.

14. **"Catching Silver Salmon on the Alagnak"** – Tips and tricks for catching silver (coho) salmon in this region.

15. **"Alaska's Sockeye Salmon: Alagnak River Hotspots"** – Popular locations and methods for sockeye fishing.

16. **"Fishing Regulations for the Alagnak River"** – Current rules and limits on fishing practices.

17. **"Catch and Release Practices on the Alagnak River"** – Ethical fishing methods for preserving fish populations.

18. **"The Economic Impact of Sport Fishing on the Alagnak River"** – How sport fishing contributes to the local economy.

Wildlife and Marine Ecosystems

19. **"The Biodiversity of the Alagnak River"** – Studies on the wide range of species that inhabit the river and its surroundings.

20. **"Marine Mammals of the Bristol Bay Region"** – Research on the seals, whales, and other marine mammals in nearby Bristol Bay.

21. **"Birds of the Alagnak River: A Birdwatcher's Guide"** – Guide to spotting bald eagles, waterfowl, and migratory birds along the river.

22. **"Bears of the Alagnak: Viewing and Conservation"** – Guide to bear behavior along the river and how to view them safely.

23. **"The Role of Salmon in the Alagnak River Ecosystem"** – How salmon migrations impact the river's ecology.

24. **"Alaska's Freshwater Fish Species: A Guide to the Alagnak"** – Overview of fish species native to the Alagnak River.

25. **"Alaska's Alagnak River as a Wildlife Corridor"** – Studies on how the river serves as a migration path for animals.

26. **"Brown Bear Activity Along the Alagnak River"** – Study on brown bear feeding patterns during salmon runs.

27. **"The Importance of Estuarine Habitats at the Alagnak River's Mouth"** – Study on estuary ecosystems and their importance to juvenile fish.

PLANT LIFE ALONG THE ALAGNAK RIVER

28. **"Riparian Vegetation of the Alagnak River"** – A study on the plant species along the river's banks.

29. **"Alaska's Boreal Forests: Flora Around the Alagnak River"** – Guide to the trees and plants that thrive in the river's environment.

30. **"Wetland Plants in the Alagnak River Delta"** – Study on the wetland plant life near the river's mouth.

31. **"Native Plant Species of Alaska's Rivers"** – Exploration of the native flora along the Alagnak.

32. **"Alaska's Tundra and River Ecosystems: A Comparative Study"** – Research comparing the tundra vegetation with riparian zones.

33. **"The Role of Sedge and Rushes in Riverbank Stability"** – Study on how these plants help prevent erosion along riverbanks.

34. **"Wildflowers Along the Alagnak River"** – Guide to identifying the wildflowers that bloom during the Alaskan summer.

35. **"Foraging for Edible Plants Along the Alagnak River"** – A guide to the edible and medicinal plants in the region.

36. **"The Impact of Invasive Plant Species on the Alagnak River's Ecosystem"** – Study on how non-native plants are affecting local flora.

37. **"Seasonal Changes in Vegetation Along the Alagnak"** – How the river's plant life changes throughout the year.

SIGHTSEEING AND ADVENTURE TOURS

38. **"Guided Rafting Tours on the Alagnak River"** – Overview of rafting trips for exploring the river's remote areas.

39. **"Helicopter Tours Over the Alagnak River"** – Guide to aerial sightseeing opportunities along the river.

40. **"Wildlife Viewing Tours on the Alagnak River"** – List of companies offering wildlife tours along the river.

41. **"Photography Tours on the Alagnak"** – Guided tours for photographers wanting to capture Alaska's wilderness.

42. **"Camping Along the Alagnak River: Tips and Spots"** – Guide to the best camping locations along the river.

43. **"Canoeing Adventures on the Alagnak River"** – Directory of canoeing routes and tour operators.

44. **"Exploring the Alagnak by Kayak"** – Guide to kayaking trips and tours along the river.

45. **"Best Scenic Spots for Wildlife Photography Along the Alagnak"** – Highlights of the most photogenic areas along the river.

46. **"Bear Viewing Tours Near the Alagnak"** – Guides to safely watching bears along the river.

47. **"Alaska's Remote Wilderness: Hiking Trails Near the Alagnak River"** – Overview of nearby hiking trails and trekking tours.

48. **"Boat Tours of the Alagnak River Delta"** – A guide to exploring the river's delta by boat.

49. **"The Best Times to Visit the Alagnak River for Wildlife"** – Seasonal guide to wildlife viewing along the river.

50. **"Fly-In Fishing and Camping Trips Along the Alagnak"** – Overview of fly-in adventures for a remote Alaskan experience.

ALAGNAK RIVER - FISHING STUDIES AND TECHNIQUES

51. **"Seasonal Fishing Patterns on the Alagnak River"** – A study on how fish behavior changes throughout the year.

52. **"Angling Techniques for Chinook Salmon on the Alagnak"** – A guide to best practices for catching Chinook salmon.

53. **"The Lifecycle of Salmon in the Alagnak River"** – Scientific study of the lifecycle of salmon species in the river.

54. **"Fly-Fishing for Grayling on the Alagnak River"** – Tips for fly-fishing one of Alaska's most popular sport fish.

55. **"Spinner Fishing for Sockeye Salmon on the Alagnak"** – Techniques for using spinning gear to catch sockeye.

56. **"The Best Time for Fishing King Salmon on the Alagnak"** – A seasonal guide to fishing for king salmon.

57. **"Nymph Fishing Techniques for Rainbow Trout on the Alagnak River"** – Strategies for fishing with nymphs in river currents.

58. **"Top Fishing Spots on the Alagnak River"** – Map and guide to the most productive fishing locations.

59. **"The Use of Artificial Flies in Alaskan Rivers"** – An overview of the best artificial flies for the Alagnak.

60. **"Fishing for Steelhead on the Alagnak: A Guide"** – Techniques and timing for catching steelhead trout.

61. **"Understanding Fish Migration in the Alagnak River"** – Scientific research on fish migration patterns.

62. **"Fishing Charters on the Alagnak: A Review"** – Directory of local charters and their services.

63. **"Catch and Release Ethics on the Alagnak River"** – Discussion on best practices for releasing fish safely.

64. **"Salmon Conservation Efforts on the Alagnak"** – Study on conservation initiatives to protect salmon populations.

65. **"Fishing Gear for the Alagnak River"** – A guide to the best fishing gear for this remote river.

66. **"Bristol Bay Fishing Lodges: Alagnak River Options"** – Overview of accommodations for anglers.

67. **"Fishing Tournaments on the Alagnak River"** – Information about competitive fishing events.

68. **"Catching Arctic Char on the Alagnak River"** – Guide to targeting this prized cold-water species.

69. **"The History of Commercial Fishing on the Alagnak River"** – Exploration of the river's role in commercial fishing.

70. **"Fly Patterns for the Alagnak River"** – The best fly patterns for catching salmon and trout.

Alagnak River Ecosystem and Environmental Studies

71. **"Alagnak River: A Biodiversity Hotspot"** – Study on the diverse species inhabiting the river ecosystem.

72. **"The Role of Riparian Zones in River Health"** – A look at the importance of riparian vegetation for the Alagnak's health.

73. **"Water Quality Monitoring in the Alagnak River"** – Ongoing studies on the water quality of the river.

74. **"Alaska's Wild Rivers: Conservation Efforts for the Alagnak"** – Overview of river conservation initiatives.

75. **"The Impact of Climate Change on the Alagnak River"** – Research on how rising temperatures are affecting river ecosystems.

76. **"Invasive Species Threats to the Alagnak River"** – A study on invasive plants and animals impacting the river.

77. **"The Role of Wetlands in the Alagnak River System"** – Research on how wetlands contribute to the river's ecosystem.

78. **"Aquatic Invertebrates of the Alagnak River"** – Study on the role of invertebrates in the river food chain.

79. **"Sediment Transport in the Alagnak River"** – Research on how sediment movement shapes the river's ecosystem.

80. **"Glacial Melt's Impact on the Alagnak River"** – Study on how glacial melting affects water levels and flow.

81. **"Beaver Activity in the Alagnak River Watershed"** – Study on the ecological effects of beaver dams along the river.

82. **"The Role of Estuaries in the Alagnak River System"** – Research on the importance of estuarine habitats for fish breeding.

83. **"Monitoring Salmon Populations on the Alagnak River"** – Methods and results from ongoing fish population surveys.

84. **"The Alagnak River as a Habitat for Endangered Species"** – Study on species at risk in the river's ecosystem.

85. **"Preserving the Wilderness of the Alagnak River"** – Overview of efforts to maintain the river's pristine conditions.

86. **"Pollution Threats to the Alagnak River"** – Research on potential pollution sources and their effects.

87. **"Fire Ecology in the Alagnak River Basin"** – Study on the impact of wildfires on the river's ecosystem.

88. **"Carbon Sequestration in Riparian Forests Along the Alagnak River"** – Research on the role of these forests in capturing carbon.

89. **"Bird Migration and the Alagnak River"** – Study on how the river serves as a key stop for migratory birds.

90. **"Fish Tagging Research on the Alagnak River"** – Overview of scientific fish tagging and tracking methods used on the river.

SIGHTSEEING AND ADVENTURE TRAVEL ON THE ALAGNAK RIVER

91. **"Float Trips on the Alagnak River"** – Guide to floating down the Alagnak on multi-day trips.

92. **"Exploring the Wilderness by Canoe: Alagnak River Routes"** – Canoeing routes and tips for navigating the river.

93. **"Alaska's Alagnak River: A Fly-In Adventure"** – Guide to fly-in tours for remote sightseeing and camping.

94. **"Scenic Flightseeing Tours Over the Alagnak River"** – Companies offering scenic flights over the river.

95. **"Camping on the Alagnak River: Remote Campsites and Tips"** – A guide to wilderness camping along the river.

96. **"Wildlife Photography on the Alagnak River"** – Best practices for photographing wildlife in the river's environment.

97. **"Exploring the Alagnak River by Raft: Adventure Tour Guide"** – Overview of rafting companies and adventure tours.

98. **"Best Seasons for Sightseeing on the Alagnak River"** – A seasonal guide to visiting the river for wildlife viewing and nature.

99. **"Exploring the Alagnak River Delta by Boat"** – Guide to exploring the river's estuary and delta by water.

100. **"Bristol Bay and the Alagnak River: A Wilderness Experience"** – Tips for combining trips to both the bay and river.

PLANT LIFE AND FLORA OF THE ALAGNAK RIVER

101. **"Alaska's Riverbank Flora: Plant Life Along the Alagnak"** – Guide to the vegetation that thrives along the riverbanks.

102. **"Riparian Plant Communities of the Alagnak River"** – Study on the different plant species that form riparian ecosystems.

103. **"Alagnak River Wetlands: A Study of Aquatic Plants"** – Research on aquatic plants that dominate the river's wetlands.

104. **"Boreal Forest Flora Around the Alagnak River"** – Overview of the boreal forest species growing in the surrounding area.

105. **"Alagnak River Tundra Ecosystems: Plant Life in the Arctic"** – Study on tundra vegetation near the river.

106. **"The Role of Willow and Alder in the Alagnak River Ecosystem"** – Research on how these plants stabilize riverbanks and provide habitat.

107. **"The Seasonal Flowering Plants of the Alagnak River"** – Guide to identifying wildflowers during the spring and summer months.

108. **"Edible Plants Along the Alagnak River"** – Overview of the edible and medicinal plants in the region.

109. **"Lichen and Moss in the Alagnak River Environment"** – Study on non-vascular plants that thrive in the moist, cold climate.

110. **"Plant Succession Patterns Along the Alagnak River"** – Research on how plant communities change over time following disturbances.

111. **"Alaska's Shrub Species: Riparian Zones of the Alagnak River"** – Guide to the shrubs found along the river.

112. **"Conservation of Native Plant Species Along the Alagnak River"** – Efforts to preserve the native plant communities.

113. **"Foraging and Wildcrafting on the Alagnak River"** – A guide to wildcrafting and foraging for food and medicinal plants.

114. **"The Impact of Flooding on Plant Life Along the Alagnak"** – Study on how seasonal flooding influences plant species.

115. **"Alaska's Cold-Climate Grasses and Their Role in Riparian Areas"** – Overview of grasses that help stabilize riverbanks in cold climates.

116. **"Invasive Plants of the Alagnak River"** – Research on the presence and control of invasive plant species.

Cultural and Indigenous Perspectives on the Alagnak River

117. **"Indigenous Knowledge and the Alagnak River"** – Study on traditional ecological knowledge

118. **"The Alagnak River in Alaska Native Culture"** – Overview of the river's importance to indigenous tribes in the region.

119. **"Subsistence Fishing Rights on the Alagnak River"** – Discussion on the legal rights of indigenous people to fish in the river.

120. **"Traditional Ecological Knowledge of the Alagnak River"** – Study on how indigenous knowledge is used for conservation and river management.

121. **"Oral Histories from the Alagnak River Tribes"** – Collection of stories and oral histories from indigenous communities.

122. **"The Role of Salmon in Indigenous Culture Along the Alagnak"** – Cultural importance of salmon for local indigenous peoples.

123. **"Indigenous Land Stewardship in the Alagnak River Basin"** – Research on the stewardship practices of native groups in the region.

124. **"Traditional Hunting and Fishing Practices Along the Alagnak River"** – Exploration of the traditional methods of hunting and fishing.

125. **"Sacred Sites and the Alagnak River"** – Overview of culturally significant locations along the river.

Wildlife Conservation and Environmental Efforts

126. **"Bear Conservation in the Alagnak River Region"** – Study on efforts to protect the bear populations that depend on the river.

127. **"Monitoring Wildlife Corridors Along the Alagnak River"** – Research on how the river acts as a wildlife corridor for large mammals.

128. **"Bristol Bay Watershed Conservation and the Alagnak River"** – Overview of watershed conservation efforts that include the Alagnak.

129. **"Conservation Success Stories from the Alagnak River"** – A collection of case studies on successful conservation initiatives.

130. **"Threats to the Alagnak River Ecosystem"** – An overview of current and future environmental threats, including climate change and pollution.

131. **"Rehabilitating Fish Populations in the Alagnak River"** – Efforts to restore declining fish populations through habitat improvement.

132. **"National Park Service Conservation Programs on the Alagnak"** – Overview of the NPS's efforts to protect the Alagnak Wild River.

133. **"Public Involvement in Conservation on the Alagnak"** – Study on community engagement in conservation initiatives along the river.

134. **"Protecting the Alagnak River from Mining Impacts"** – Research on the potential environmental impacts of mining in the region.

135. **"Salmon Habitat Restoration Projects on the Alagnak"** – Study of restoration projects aimed at improving salmon spawning areas.

Plant Life and Ecology Along the Alagnak River

136. **"Plant Adaptations to Cold Climates in the Alagnak River Region"** – Study on how plants adapt to the cold, wet conditions along the river.

137. **"Vegetation Zonation Along the Alagnak River"** – Research on how plant communities are distributed based on elevation and water availability.

138. **"Ecological Succession in Floodplain Habitats of the Alagnak River"** – Study on how floodplain habitats regenerate after disturbances.

139. **"Alaska's Riparian Forests: The Alagnak River's Role"** – Research on the river's impact on the surrounding riparian forest ecosystems.

140. **"Aquatic Plant Life in the Alagnak River"** – Overview of the aquatic plants that grow in the river itself and their ecological roles.

141. **"The Role of Fungi in the Alagnak River's Ecosystem"** – Study on the symbiotic relationships between fungi and plants in the river's environment.

142. **"Tundra Flora Near the Alagnak River"** – Overview of the tundra vegetation in the higher elevations surrounding the river.

143. **"Cold Climate Wildflowers: Alagnak River Region"** – Guide to identifying wildflowers that thrive in the river's cold environment.

Sightseeing and Ecotourism on the Alagnak River

144. **"Eco-Friendly Tours on the Alagnak River"** – Companies offering sustainable tourism experiences.

145. **"The Alagnak River as a Destination for Nature Lovers"** – Guide to what makes the river a prime spot for eco-tourism.

146. **"Exploring the Alagnak by Canoe: Ecotourism and Wildlife"** – An in-depth look at eco-tours focused on wildlife viewing by canoe.

147. **"Best Campsites Along the Alagnak River"** – Guide to the most scenic and accessible camping spots along the river.

Alagnak River Geology and Physical Environment

Adventure and Wilderness Exploration

159. **"Packrafting the Alagnak River: A Wilderness Guide"** – Overview of the gear and routes for packrafting along the river.

160. **"Kayaking Adventures in the Alagnak River's Tributaries"** – A guide to exploring the smaller tributaries feeding into the Alagnak.

161. **"Exploring Remote Parts of the Alagnak River: Off the Beaten Path"** – A guide to more remote, less traveled areas of the river.

162. **"Multi-Day Rafting Expeditions on the Alagnak"** – Tour operators offering multi-day rafting trips on the river.

Captain Rami Geffner, MD's strong affinity and fondness for the ocean has been a steadfast presence throughout his life. From an early age, Rami accompanied his father on a number of sailing trips, where he fell in love with everything about the sea. He now plans and sets out on his own seafaring adventures and is involved with the local maritime community. Rami holds a bachelor's degree in biology, a master's in human anatomy from Rutgers University, a medical degree from the New Jersey School of Medicine, and as well as multiple degrees in Dermatopathology. Rami continues to practice Dermatology, Dermatopathology and Mohs surgery in Pennsylvania and New Jersey. This is his third book.